What a
Modern Catholic
Believes About
EUCHARIST

by John Krump

the thomas more press
chicago illinois

Permission to use quotations from *A Contemporary Theology of Grace*
by Charles Meyer, Copyright 1970 by Alba House, Staten Island, N.Y.,
is gratefully acknowledged.

Standard Book Number: 0-88347-040-3

TABLE OF CONTENTS

Chapter 1

IN ILLO TEMPORE

I GREW UP in an age when church was where you went, not what you were. *In illo tempore*[1] we went up to the house of the Lord, not always rejoicing exactly, but with what in retrospect seems an astonishing frequency. Of course, mass on Sundays and holy days of obligation was understandably popular. In those days the church didn't mess around with how you felt about going or whether it meant anything: missing mass was, for practical purposes, unthinkable. The obligation was there all right, but it was normally no great burden and we would have righteously (and rightly, I think) denied that our going every Sunday was merely or mainly a matter of obligation. The truth was we usually had good feelings during mass and always afterwards. Besides, except for an invisible cadre of lapsed Catholics whom we prayed would be reclaimed by the annual mission, everyone, it seemed, went. Sunday mass was as normal as Sunday dinner.

The church claimed impressive multitudes, however, at many other times besides Sunday mornings. First Fridays were felt to be only slightly less sacred than the sabbath and, on the strength of the testimony of St. Margaret Mary, considerably more productive, at least if you managed nine in

7

a row. Lenten weekdays brought many people to mass, as did special feast days like St. Patrick's when black vestments were replaced by white (or green). But, unlike now, mass was by no means the only nor for many the most satisfying staple on our liturgical menu. We had a wide variety of offerings, many of which would be unpalatable now but at that time kept a lot of people coming back for more. Many parents made confession a weekly ritual for their children, only slightly less necessary than the Saturday night bath; and perhaps a majority of adults had been taught that, state of grace or not, confession was a *sine qua non* for going to Communion. Then there was the Tuesday or Friday evening novena and a host of seasonal delights: St. Blaise Day, Ash Wednesday, Stations of the Cross, a strange rite on Lenten Sunday afternoons called Vespers, the rousing Good Friday Tre Ore, Forty Hours, May Crowning, and that wondrous day in early November when you went to three Masses (45 minutes) and made six staccato visits later in the day to bail out one of the Poor Souls in Purgatory. Except for the summer when church going was confined to the narrower ambiance of mass and confession, there was always something special coming up. Church was where you went—often.

Of course, church was not only a building, it was something we were "in," "belonged to." It was the Roman Catholic Church, the "only true Church," founded by God not men, "one, holy, catholic, and apostolic." Other churches might have had one or other of the "marks," but only the Catholic church had all four. It was all so simple, so transparent; while hoping invincible ignorance applied to my Lutheran buddies, I marveled at its very possibility. To be sure, we were frequently admonished that our being Catholic was a sign of God's predilection, the direct effect of his special providence in our behalf. That, however, was an element of the kerygma that gave rise to my first feeble doubt, or rather "difficulty," as we were wont to call such things in those days. Didn't my parents being Catholic have anything to do with my good fortune? Still, it was a nice church—no bare, ruined choir—to belong to.

The fact that ours was the largest church in the neighborhood; that like American Family Soap we didn't even have to advertise because all but the early masses were crowded and the later ones standing room only; that our church had doctrines, confession, saints, devotion to Mary, Friday abstinence—everything a church ought to have—all convinced us that we Catholics occupied a superior position under heaven. What really anchored the whole system, however, was papal infallibility which meant in the existential order that what the church, from pope to priest, said *had* to be true because in reality it was God speaking, or rather, giving orders. Commitment to the church, thus, yielded nothing less than metaphysical and moral certitude. True enough, a mortal sin was a mortal sin, was a mortal sin, was a mortal sin; but confession would handle that difficulty and an act of perfect contrition could tide you over until you got there. Certainly, the church allowed us poor sinners few illusions about our sanctity; nonetheless, we took no little pride in belonging to a church that was perfect, that had never changed nor ever would, that never erred nor ever could. For one thing it gave you a distinct feeling of being "one up" in any ecumenical interchange. I recall one such debate with a Lutheran friend at age eleven when I concluded my argument with the smug assertion: "We Catholics don't *believe* in Purgatory, we *know!*" Such an assertion was in no way a denial of the opacity of the supernatural but rather evidence of a robust, if naive, confidence in the teaching authority of the church. In your heart you knew they were right—always.

We know differently now, of course. Contemporary theologians have pointed out the disastrous results of substituting law and authority for grace: religion is rationalized, the power of word and sacrament blunted. The people of God become God's sheep and, little by little, just sheep. Vatican II has begun to reverse the process but the sad heritage of many centuries is not easily shrugged off. The point here, though, is that, amid the steady thrust toward rationalization, the liturgy, as bad as it was on so many counts, managed to serve as a saving, if not amazing, grace.

We sensed some of this in a vague way even as children. What really mattered ultimately was the life of grace, or better, "being in the state of grace," which required not just knowing the teachings of the Catholic Church but living by them. And this we knew in a decidedly experiential way was impossible without being close to God. And where was God to be found? In church, of course, in the Blessed Sacrament, there to listen to our problems and petitions, receive our acts of faith, hope, love, and contrition, and give us grace. This stupendous fact, symbolized by the lonely red sanctuary lamp that burned night and day, was in the last analysis the decisive reason why any Catholic church had it all over the most splendid of Protestant churches. In their churches, Protestants only had something called "Divine Worship;" we had something infinitely better, Divine Presence.

This is not to suggest that the mass was not important in those days. We didn't view it as a "celebration of life," "the act of the Christian community," still less as a "sacred meal." It was the "holy sacrifice of the mass," the sacred mystery, which regardless of its setting, outdoors on a battlefield, tiny country chapel, or gorgeous basilica, infallibly delivered God into our midst. *Hoc est enim corpus meum!* No wonder we never wondered that at mass we spoke not a word, spent most of the hour on our knees, and tried, save for the consecration when we were alerted by the bells, to occupy ourselves with prayerbook or rosary and prepare ourselves for the supreme moment of Holy Communion. That His advent should be announced and effected in Latin (foreign language) by a priest (special person) wearing vestments (sacred clothes) using bread and wine (specified materials) seemed altogether appropriate. We wouldn't have associated God with the ordinary. That we couldn't understand or even hear most of the words nor interpret the meaning of the gestures had a positive value. It enhanced our sense of mystery. Besides, the mass was the priest's privilege. We were there to watch and adore Him when He came and, thanks to Pius X, receive Him in Holy Communion.

It seems safe to say that going to Communion was what made mass worthwhile in those days. While mass did offer a sacred time and place for saying prayers, as a total experience it left not a little to be desired. It seemed endless and continually outran my repertoire of prayers long before the time for Communion arrived. I can still remember the blessed feeling of relief at the prospect of imminent release when the priest whipped into the cadence of the Leonine prayers: "O God, our refuge and our strength." Not much relief was provided by what followed the Gospel except that we got to sit down. This sequence invariably began with an announcement of the Sunday or Feast Day, even on Christmas and Easter when you would have thought everybody knew. Next were prayers for recently deceased members of the parish, perhaps a proclamation of a special collection, a briefing on upcoming parish activities, and a recital of all the mass intentions including the donors for the ensuing week. All this was followed by the reading of the Gospel in the vernacular and frequently, though not always and seldom in the summer, a sermon. The latter I tended to view as an unfortunate lengthening of the mass, an unnecessary interruption that delayed the solemn moments of Consecration and Communion. It wasn't that I suffered from what J. F. Powers called "my Sunday sickness." I liked sermons at "Rosary, Sermon, and Benediction," or at "Lenten Devotions," or "The Tre Ore;" but never on Sunday. Sacrament was enough.

In that connection, it is instructive to recall that in the old days for the congregation, the ushers, servers, priest— everyone, in fact, except the choir—good liturgy was marked by a certain dispatch. The vernacular expression employed by the clergy and the ushers was "getting them out." I recall with a kind of perverse admiration the story of a rather famous monsignor who on Holy Thursday after a solemn mass, a procession that included 150 second graders, a large posse of altar boys, and at least three trips through the *Pange Lingua*, swept into the sacristy, looked at his watch and beamed, "67 minutes—not bad!" Of course, on the view that the mass is really only infallible ritual machinery for producing the Blessed Sacrament, he was right. That was the great thing about the mass; it *worked* no matter what. Reverence and faith were institutionalized in ritual. So, quite understandably, the desired tempo was *allegro con moto* with a cut back to *adagio* at the words of consecration.

These were the magic words; this was what the mass was all about. Bread and wine became the body and blood of Christ. Jesus, not my brother, but "my Lord and my God," really and truly was resting upon the altar, soon to be (if it were not a wedding or funeral mass) the "Divine Guest" in my soul. Reverently, I closed my eyes and received the host on my tongue. Unsure as to just how transubstantiation made him present in the host, I scrupulously avoided contact with my teeth as well as the alternate horror of getting the host stuck on the roof of my mouth. Its recovery from that position made it seem like you were chewing the host, which was viewed as ostentatious, irreverent, or both. Anyway, I wanted to make Jesus comfortable and get the host down so we could talk. Well instructed by the Sisters, I generally followed up my initial welcome with a *pro forma* thanksgiving for the sanctifying grace he was dropping off as well as all the actual graces that would be available through the week as needed. In our conversation, which sometimes went on for several minutes, I normally did most of the talking; but I had the pleasant sense of being heard. When Communion had been particularly fervent, it made the experience of mass seem very good indeed. Better yet, as Frank O'Connor put it in one of his stories, it produced "the feeling of strangeness which lasted throughout the whole day and reduced reality to its proportions. . . . You don't mind it so much if you get a hammering. You know there's something else in the world besides the hammering."

Pointing out the limitations of the Eucharistic piety of our formative years, theologians have lamented the "reification" of the Eucharist, the tendency to view the Blessed Sacrament as a sacred *thing* rather than as a sign of the personal presence of Jesus. The truth of this indictment comes clear when one remembers the exaggerated measures the church prescribed to insure "reverence" for the sacred species. After the Consecration the celebrant's "canonical fingers" (thumb and forefinger) had to be kept together until after the ablutions lest some miniscule fragments of the host be dropped and profaned. Following Communion, the corporal was carefully scoured for the same reason. The patens received the same careful treatment. Cloths that came into contact with the species required a lavabo by the priest before they were released to the sister sacristan for ordinary laundering. When a host was dropped at the communion rail an emergency procedure went into effect. The server froze in his tracks and the priest hurried to the altar to fetch a little cloth with which he covered the spot after retrieving the host. If, worst of all, the host fell from your tongue onto your hands or clothes, you had a sense of ritual impurity the rest of the day. It was a chance you took when you went to Communion. Fortunately, it didn't happen very often.

In this connection, one should not forget the severity of the Eucharistic fast even on the occasion of First Communion. Catechesis for this solemn event invariably ended with baleful stories of other children who had gotten up the night before for a drink or who had brushed their teeth and swallowed one drop of water and thus lost their chance. One's family was to be mobilized to head off any such tragedy: tooth brush removed from its normal place, bathroom glass plugged with Kleenex. It was a little hard to look forward with joy to receiving Jesus for the first time when it was so easy to disqualify yourself.

Now I bring all this up neither to laugh at nor lament the passing of Catholicism of yesteryear. The focus of this book is the Eucharist which in its meaning and manner of celebration has been and will always be an accurate reflection of what the church is believed to be at that time. The church makes the Eucharist and Eucharist makes the church—for better or worse. That relationship and its historicity are truths that have been recovered in recent years. Both will be explored in succeeding chapters. But the point here is not simply to recall the Eucharist of our childhood and wonder at the enormity of the change over the past decade in particular, but precisely to remember that that was the Eucharist of our *childhood* and to reflect on the uncommon importance of that fact. It obviously suggests understanding if not approval of those who have rejected liturgical development on the simple grounds that it was a departure from what they knew and believed to be right. But it intimates something more. Might it not be useful for those who have more or less cheerfully, even eagerly, accepted the changes since Vatican II and yet currently are enjoying it less to probe more deeply for the origins of that disaffection? New wine has to be stored in new wineskins.

Let us explore the point at some length. Consider the sequence of the developments in Eucharistic practice over the past three decades. Though lay participation in the liturgy had been called for by Pius X as far back as 1903 and reiterated later with some disclaimers by Pius XI, it seems fair to say that few took their words seriously. Undoubtedly there was not a little reluctance on the part of the clergy to allow the laity to enter what had been their private preserve for centuries. More than that, the liturgy was not a prime pastoral concern. Sure it was important to have, but the priest's sole contribution to its efficacy was the "proper intention." That, of course, was the wonderful thing about the mass and the sacraments: they worked by themselves—auto-

matically. They were sacred ceremonies, set in every significant detail, not to be tampered with. Priestly efforts were to
be directed elsewhere.

Still the spirit was abroad in the land and there appeared
Father Stedman's missal. In my view, it marked the definitive beginning of popular liturgical development, a small but
enormously satisfying change. It was inexpensive, illustrated,
and its ingenious numbering system made the dialogue mass
feasible if the pastor deigned or dared to have it. However,
with or without the dialogue mass it gave the mass-bound
Catholic a better deal. At the very least you had something
now to do there, a task to accomplish that enhanced the
satisfaction of having gone to mass. More than that, we
found the mass prayers, at least some of them, astonishingly
beautiful. The taut objectivity of the prayers of the Roman
liturgy and the snippets of the psalms and other parts of
Scripture were a refreshing change from the sweeter, subjective piety of the Catholic Girls Guide and the like, and
eventually, it seems, modified popular taste in prayers. Even
more, having a missal was not a little like having an official
score card. It brought you into the action so to speak, allowed you to be united with the priest. It offered the opportunity of saying, privately at least, the best prayer, the official
prayer of the Catholic Church. With the missal the mass became, in Louis Putz's phrase, "my mass." It was a desirable
change and hard come by in the sense that it required considerable effort at least by a few. Yet the mass hadn't
changed; it was the same semimagical, otherworldly reality
as before. Nor was there much inclination even within the
Liturgical Movement to seek basic changes. The problem—
it was generally though not universally felt—lay not with the

mass itself but in the fact that the people had been dealt out of it for so long. All that was needed was a campaign to secure their active participation. Thus Dom Remberg Sorg, O.S.B., at the 1944 National Liturgical Week in Chicago concluded a long argument against an English liturgy with the assertion: "It is quite unnecessary from the standpoint of active participation, and altogether regrettable for disciplinary and theological reasons, to substitute a vernacular for the Latin of our Roman Liturgy." The language problem could be overcome, he and others suggested, by the introduction of two years of Latin in parochial schools. Man was for the Latin liturgy, not the other way around, just like Jesus said.

During the late fifties, active participation caught on more and more. Hundreds of parishes across the country began to pray (quickly) and sing (slowly) together at least at one mass on Sunday. We learned about the structure of the mass from Father Clifford Howell's immensely popular *Of Sacraments and Sacrifice:* we talk to God; he talks to us; we give God a gift; he gives it back to us. The mass was not a prayer but an action, a sacrifice, which was not like giving up something for Lent, but sharing a box of candy with God. Understandably many Catholics reacted positively, a point that Father John Jankauskas attempted to document in a study he made of a Back-of-the-Yards parish in Chicago. Typical was the following response:

> [Active participation] gave the Mass a deep meaning. Now I understand much more clearly. This never would have been possible without the recited Mass. . . . That's when I really got honestly excited. For the first time in my life, I wanted to learn what the Mass really is.[2]

While the relentless spread of the recited and sung mass bred excitement in most quarters, the focus of the latter varied. CFM groups made getting a dialogue mass into their parishes an "action." But converts to the Stedman missal who had moved up to a large daily missal resented being asked to let off tracking the priest and sing an offertory hymn. It seemed like a regression. The communion song, for obvious reasons, drew especially stiff resistance. Some pastors continued to hold out, labeling the burgeoning movement as a silly or even dangerous fad; some parishioners made it a point to avoid the masses with active participation; some choirs suffered sullen resistance, failed to adapt, then folded. But interest in the reinvigorated liturgy whipped on by priests and others whose admirable enthusiasm was not always encumbered by theological critique continued to grow.

Still, at this point nothing very drastic had changed. Though now we no longer merely belonged to the church, we *were* the church, the revolutionary implications of the new rhetoric could not have been expected to be understood within a few short years; nor were they. The church was the same, gifted in recent years with magnificent Popes, conservative but not rigid, growing in power and favor with its own members and with the public at large. Nor had there occurred any real change in the Eucharist. Active participation had become the rule rather than the exception. The Eucharistic fast had long since disappeared and after a struggle the daily morning requiem. Evening mass was becoming more common. But none of these changes really affected us very deeply. In fact, our convictions about the power of the Eucharist, though more subtly expressed, were livelier than ever. By the time of Vatican II some at least were ready for thoroughgoing liturgical reforms. If and when they took place, it was felt, the Parousia would dawn, *instanter*. The novena would at last have been expunged and the whole Church would rejoice, united in love at the table of the Lord, then go forth to "restore all things in Christ."

A lot of things have happened since Vatican II; but despite massive liturgical reform the Parousia is not one of them. Far from being united in love around the table of the Lord, Catholics are increasingly absent from mass. A significantly smaller percentage of American Catholics goes to mass weekly now than did in 1963, the year the *Constitution on the Sacred Liturgy* was promulgated. As one wag put it, "The problem with the Mass now is that nobody is going." Not a few who do are just desperately hanging on.

It seems true enough to say that more reforms must come. It is even more to the point to suggest we could do a lot better with what we've got. But it is, I think, absolutely crucial to insist that our prime concern ought to be liturgical *renewal*, which, if Vatican II is to be taken seriously, is coterminous with Christian renewal in the most profound sense of the word. This will involve more than further tinkering with rites or the restoration of Benediction and other atavisms. Not the least important elements of that renewal will be our coming to appreciate what the Church is and what it is not, what the Eucharist can do and what it can't. A sign that the radical word Vatican II offered about both questions has been rightly understood is a quiet, untroubled awareness that its word is not the last word. And that, I would suggest, is a much harder problem for all of us than we would first think.

Chapter 2

FROM THE UPPER ROOM TO
ST. URSULA[1]

"ONE OF the great difficulties we have in understanding the meaning of the Church, or indeed the meaning of any aspect of Christianity," writes Andrew Greeley, "is the impression that most of us obtained during our formative years that everything was settled. There were no unsolved theological questions in the Church . . . everything that needed to be said was said."[2] In those formative years, it was suggested earlier, the notion that "everything was settled," far from being a source of dissatisfaction, was precisely the thing that made the church wonderful and great in our eyes. We took enormous pride and, not to our credit, great comfort in belonging to a church that had it all together from the very beginning. Just being a Catholic, of course, didn't guarantee salvation; but, unlike the rest of mankind, you certainly knew the way. All you needed to do was add minimal performance. There were no further questions, no surprises. Our church always was and always would be.

No wonder a cry of horror went up in many quarters when the faithful got a look at the New Mass. It really was different. The mass had changed, the significance of which was sensed at least by most Catholics: maybe the church had a history after all. The awful secret of Vatican II was out.

The realization that the church is historical, not just in the sense of having its ups and downs as a result of extrinsic forces, but that it has changed, will change, indeed *must* change, that it has to grope for appropriate expression of itself in every succeeding age, to say the least, considerably alters one's theological perspective. The New Mass becomes merely the newest mass. What it means to us, how it succeeds or fails comes clearer though only when we remember where we've been and how we got there. What follows, therefore, is a brief sojourn through the history of the Eucharist from the Upper Room to St. Ursula.

That what happened in the Upper Room on the night before Jesus died and what was happening every Sunday, in fact, every morning at St. Ursula's were firmly identified in our minds clearly testifies to the abiding presence of the Holy Spirit in the church. With Paul VI in *Mysterium Fidei,* therefore, we might very well "rejoice in the faith of the Church which has always been one and the same" despite significant shifts in theological perspective and in the manner of celebration. All the same, it does seem incredible that we never wondered why the two looked so very different. I mean we knew what our mass looked like (if not what it meant) and from prints of the DaVinci painting we knew (we thought) what the Last Supper looked like: Jesus seated at the center of a long banquet table with the Apostles ranged around him. It might have been instructive had we asked that question a long time ago.

At any rate, the shape of the mass has been changing ever since the beginning, though the greatest development took place through the first six centuries of the church. The beginning, of course, was the Last Supper which according to most scholars was probably the passover or paschal supper for Jesus and his disciples. Some difficulty in chronology exists between the synoptics and John, but it seems likely that, if the night on which the supper occurred was not Passover at least it was *their* passover meal, rather like families who anticipate or postpone Thanksgiving dinner in order to accommodate some relatives. More will be said about the paschal supper and its origins in a later chapter but here it is important to note that this first "mass" was not a brand new rite that Jesus sprang on his apostles. Like other devout Jewish communities or families they had celebrated together not only the annual passover meal but the weekly chaburah, a sabbath evening meal that was simpler than the passover but also included a ritual sharing of bread and wine along with a special prayer of thanksgiving and praise (berakah) after which the Christian eucharistic prayer is modeled. Undoubtedly, it would be something like a dozen of us having a warm, informal home mass with the bishop every week. Even more meaningful must have been the meals the Apostles ate with Jesus after his resurrection. To a group of Gentiles assembled at the house of Cornelius, Peter enthuses, "Now we are those witnesses—we have eaten and drunk with him after his resurrection from the dead" (Acts 10:41). All this gives us a little idea not only of what the Apostles and others who came to believe in Jesus *did* when they came together for the "breaking of the bread" or the "Lord's Supper," which Christians later called the "Eucharist" and still later "missa" (mass), but what this communal action *meant* to them. The Risen Lord was alive and with them and they felt this most acutely when they gathered to celebrate his supper.

It should be added immediately that Paul helped uncover the meaning of the supper Jesus had told his followers to repeat in his memory. "The blessing-cup that we bless is a communion with the blood of Christ, and the bread that we break is a communion with the body of Christ" (I Cor. 10:16). Through that communion with the body and blood of Christ, "though there be many of us, we form a single body" (I Cor. 10:17). Through the Eucharist, those baptized, incorporated into the body of Jesus, proclaimed that identity with him and deepened it. All of the seemingly endless exhortations to fraternal love in the letters of Paul are to be understood in the light of this reality. In a real sense for Paul, love is no longer a commandment but a corollary, or rather, a consequence of the Christian's identity with Christ. And this is what the early Christians celebrated in the Eucharist. No wonder they were such joyous celebrations.

Though the New Testament yields few specific details about these early Eucharists, it does offer some general information. We know that initially, as one might expect, Christians met to celebrate the Eucharist in the evening and that very early they chose the first day of the Jewish week, the day of the Resurrection, as their sabbath, which, because the day was reckoned in the Jewish manner, meant those early masses took place on Saturday evening. The Eucharist was normally accompanied by an agape, a fraternal meal which for a short time separated the blessing and sharing of the bread from that of the cup as was the case at the Last Supper. Very early, however, the two rites were brought together at the end of the meal and the Eucharist more clearly assumed its specifically Christian character. Gradually the meal disappeared as communities continued to grow; and both factors led to a move from homes to some kind of community hall as the place of assembly and a joining of the evening Eucharist with Sunday morning service of readings and prayers patterned after the Jewish synagogue service which Christians had stopped frequenting as the gap between the two communities widened. A subtler change occurred with the former move. The Eucharist became, necessarily, a more stylized ritual meal: people stood instead of reclining, the focus was more on the table than the community, even its name changed. It was the Didache, an early Christian document from the turn of the century in which the word "Eucharist" first appears.

Nonetheless, the communitarian emphasis remained paramount both in the experience and the theology of the Eucharist which began to be developed by the Fathers. Ignatius of Antioch, for instance, wrote vigorously about the bishop as the image and safeguard of the essential unity of the church that was expressed in eucharistic celebration. It was the bishop assisted by presbyters and deacons, who presided over the one Eucharist of the community; and only later when the sheer number of Christians made more celebrations necessary were local parishes established with priests ordained to serve them precisely as representatives of the bishop. A lovely rite sprung up to express the unity of these subcommunities: a particle of the consecrated bread from the bishop's Eucharist was brought to the outlying parishes and dropped into the cup during their Eucharist.

With regard to the form of the Eucharist, the early centuries in particular offer a picture of more or less freewheeling development together with a trend toward consolidation and standardization. About the year 150, *The First Apology* of Justin mentions readings, the kiss of peace, mixing wine and water, and a eucharistic prayer proclaimed by the presiding minister, to which all responded "Amen." *The Apostolic Traditions* of St. Hippolytus, an important early third-century document, evidences the existence of the preface dialogue and an early canon whose recovery caused not a little excitement recently. After the Edict of Milan when the church was no longer a network of small if spreading communities perpetually in danger of government harrassment (but the quite visible "city of God" that claimed the Emperor as a believer), it had more time and taste for liturgical development. In an exultant mood over their new freedom, Christians built churches that looked like Roman government buildings (basilicas) which Jungman notes "had a forepart shaped to resemble a throne room, God's throne to which his people have access and to which they stream in their multitudes led by rows of pillars to the nave."[3] By the end of the century the core of the Roman canon was intact, Christmas, Epiphany and other feasts were added to a developing liturgical year, and liturgical books for the celebrant, lectors, and singers made their appearance. Even though at this point there was still considerable room for improvisation even in the eucharistic prayer, the basic framework of the mass was set.

Tradition died somewhat easier in those days. In 384, Pope Damasus I scrapped Greek for Latin as the liturgical language of the western church. Though it may have been a hundred years late, the move was important: it put the liturgy in the language of the people. This change in language assumes considerable historical interest when one remembers that the next time it occurred in the Latin rite was December 4, 1963.

By the middle of the 6th century, the liturgy had developed enough to have its first official reform at the hands of Gregory the Great, who reputedly "cut many things, changed a few, and added some." The form of Pope Gregory's "new mass" would not have surprised us even in our St. Ursula days but the spirit and mode of celebration most certainly would have. Though the Roman liturgy was solemn, even stately, enriched by new prayers, chants, and gestures, its basic structure and significance had not been occluded. The people stood close to the altar and to their bishop; their "Amens" as St. Jerome said, still resounded like a peal of heavenly thunder. Their Eucharist was still the celebration of the community of Jesus Christ "proclaiming his death until he comes."

However, whether or not the Roman liturgy around 600 was, as some claim, the "mass at its best," a question had arisen in the East whose answer and counter-answer made the next five centuries the period of perhaps the greatest revolution in religious thought and practice that the Church has ever seen. That revolution was very much alive at St. Ursula; its spirit, I would suggest, lives still. The question Jesus had long before put to Peter, "Who do you say I am?" had been answered rightly. However, before the New Testament period was over, some Christians were interpreting his answer differently enough for John to seek to counteract in his gospel. Heterodox answers continued to spawn various "isms" which different Fathers struggled against with uneven results until a priest by the name of Arius flatly denied the divinity of Christ. The Council of Chalcedon in 451 flattened Arius with its famous dogmatic formula "verus Deus et verus homo,"[4] ever after which the church tended to forget what followed the "et." Still the spirit of Arius went marching on with the Teutonic tributes through the west where the battle was fought all over again and ended only with the conversion of the Spanish Visigothic King Rekkared and his Arian constituents to the Catholic Church in 589. What didn't end was the intense bitterness stirred up during the century of Arian conquest and the almost hysterical determination to attack anything that remotely smacked of the heresy.

So the West, like the East before it, though with different results, became relentlessly anti-Arian both in theological perspective and liturgical practice. Christ disappeared into the Trinity, the doctrine of which during the years of strife had become the theological bulwark for the divinity of the former and the battlecry of orthodoxy. Heaven and earth thus separated; the cult of Mary and (later) of the saints emerged to fill the void. As for the church, the biological metaphor which portrayed "her" as the fruitful mother whose womb (the baptismal font) constantly brought forth the sons of God yielded to a juridical, authoritative image. All this had a pronounced impact on the self-image of the average Christian. His association with the redeeming humanity of Jesus obscured, he became a poor, worthless sinner who had to pray hard and desperately to win graces[5] for salvation.

In the liturgy the anti-Arian reaction prompted a change in the character of Sunday from an Easter renewal to a Feast of the Trinity. The Nicene Creed became standard; the *Suscipe Sancta Trinitas* and *Placeat* prayers were introduced; and the *Kyrie eleison,* formerly a Christological acclamation, was given a Trinitarian twist. Other changes which more appropriately expressed the distance between the people and God on the altar gradually took hold: confessions of unworthiness, silent recitation of the canon, multiple signs of the cross over the gifts, variations in the Communion procedure. The faithful no longer went to the table of the Lord where they stood to receive but to the altar rail where they knelt. Preoccupation with reverence, clean hands, and possible misuse of the Eucharist led to the abandonment of the nine-centuries-old practice of receiving Communion in one's hands. About the same time the use of leavened bread was discontinued and two centuries later Communion under both species disappeared.

What had disappeared from the Communion rite much earlier was the laity. The situation was bad enough to prompt the Fourth Lateran Council in 1215 to legislate annual communion under pain of mortal sin, a law that still enjoyed some relevance in our St. Ursula days.

New interest in the Eucharist was prompted by the Carolingian reforms which ushered in the Middle Ages; though at this point the old anti-Arian reaction was too deep, too much a part of the ordinary Christian consciousness to be even recognized let alone reversed. Still, by the end of the Middle Ages things had grown more cheerful. People flocked into various Blessed Sacrament confraternities which were forever sponsoring pilgrimages and processions. By the eve of the Reformation, with a church or two on every block, an enormous number of clerics, and at least 50 Feast Days a year, there was a lot of liturgy around, much of it festive, colorful, often accompanied by drama, and—well—entertaining. It was also felt to be efficacious. A brisk traffic in stipends went on with masses multiplied to accommodate the demands of the faithful. Eucharistic piety was expressed not by participation but by watching. It was common for people to run from altar to altar to glimpse the host at the elevation. Efforts at reforms never really had a chance. Magic had replaced mystery.

The Council of Trent could hardly have been expected to turn it all around and it didn't. Lacking research, working in a very sensitive political situation, hoping to head off further losses and at the same time pull the church together, the council fathers nonetheless managed to eliminate the worst horrors of a decadent liturgy as well as hammer out a comprehensive and fairly well balanced statement of the theology of the Eucharist. Ultimately, however, Trent failed, not so much because its concrete reforms fell short of what was needed, but mostly because it did not restore that integrated biblical vision of Christ, church, and Eucharist which might have succeeded in vitalizing the church. In effect, its temperate measures delayed radical reform and renewal for the next four centuries. Just a few years later, Pius V's reform of the missal and breviary utilized the technology of printing to impose an unprecedented standardization of the liturgy that ushered in what has been called the "Age of Rubrics."

However, during the Baroque era, the spirit of St. Ursula emerged more clearly. It was as though after a century of turmoil, defeat, and defections the Catholic Church braced by the taut discipline that Trent had injected everywhere, picked itself up and rejoiced that it was alive, that it had been faithful. It still had the Pope, the Mass, the Real Presence, and Mary. A nervous triumphalism that lasted pretty much intact until Vatican II began to take hold. Piety quickened; this was the age that gave us the Feast of Corpus Christi, Forty Hours, Benediction, and evening devotions that united Marian and Eucharistic cult. But it tended to be a sweet, subjective spirituality because it was not centered in the mass but rather sprung up around it. Trent had not really unlocked the mass nor returned it to the people.

In the ensuing years some tried, and failed. In 17th-century France a splendid liturgical revival spearheaded by some remarkably gifted churchmen never really got off the ground. Unfortunately, it tended to be identified in both the popular and papal mind with Jansenism, Protestantism or both. Wrote Pope Alexander VII in 1661:

> We have learned with great sorrow that in the Kingdom of France, certain sons of perdition, itching with novelties, detrimental to souls, and despising the laws and practices of the church, have lately come to such madness as to dare to translate the Roman Missal into French, and hand it over to persons of every rank and sex . . . thus to degrade, lower the mystery, and expose the divine mysteries to common gaze.[6]

About fifty years later a French missal with the Great Amen printed in red was proscribed. Thus the mass, the "official public worship of the church" as Canon Law called it, remained important but oddly peripheral, simply "one of the five ways of honoring the Blessed Sacrament" as the Catechism of Wuerzburg of 1734 said. For the devout, in a way, it came to represent sacred time. Thus St. Francis DeSales, when about to be consecrated a bishop, made a resolution always to say his beads when his duties required him to attend a public mass. That little incident says very much, indeed, about what the mass has meant to perhaps most Catholics from Trent until our own time.

It does not say it all, however. At St. Ursula's some things had changed. We made our First Communion in second grade, which was a departure from what had been the custom in our parents' day. As children we were expected to avail ourselves of the privilege at least weekly. Adults received less often partly because at that time the rigorous eucharistic fast was still intact. Yet they were encouraged to receive frequently since it was a "good example" for their children as well as an important spiritual benefit for themselves—"a monthly investment in eternity," as our Holy Name men used to be reminded. And we had Gregorian Chant (or something like it) which we were to hold in awe because it was the *official* music of the Catholic Church. These improvements, such as they were, are to be credited to Pius X who had the benefit of the scholarship and experience of a modern liturgical movement that had been growing in momentum in Europe for more than a half-century. As children, however, we could hardly grasp the significance of these changes. That my parents made their First Communion at age fourteen, that they were admonished never to receive without first going to confession seemed considerably less remarkable and far less interesting than the fact that horses were more popular than automobiles in their day. For us life changed, but not the liturgy, not the church. It was easy for us to identify the Upper Room with St. Ursula. The sequence of events through the past 1300 years, however, had made it almost impossible for us to clarify that identity or recognize the difference.

That, with Vatican II, is possible. But not easy. For the task is no longer one of merely authenticating the present, but of responsibly shaping the future. The church, we now say, is not static but dynamic; it is always becoming. The same is true of our understanding and celebration of Eucharist.

However, the above historical overview was not simply to indicate where and why we went wrong in the past but to intimate the enormous difficulty of really turning things around. The Carolingian reform merely touched the extremes of the anti-Arian reaction; Trent never really got at the root of the liturgical decadence of the late Middle Ages. By all counts Vatican II has done infinitely better. But theological documents and liturgical reforms are one thing; their appropriation by the church as a whole is another. Toward the latter purpose the words of Paul seem relevant: "God's gift was not a spirit of timidity, but the Spirit of power, and love, and self-control" (Tim. 1:7).

Chapter 3

PROCLAMATION OF THE MYSTERY

. . . He has let us know the mystery of his purpose, the hidden plan he so kindly made in Christ from the beginning to act upon when the times had run their course to the end: that he would bring everything together under Christ, as head, everything in the heavens and everything on earth. . . .
Ephesians 1:9–10.

THERE IS a lot to be said for the expression Catholics most commonly use for the Eucharist—Holy Communion. It best describes the ultimate meaning of Eucharist, of the church, of the Christian religion itself, which is nothing less than "communion with God among men"[1] through incorporation in Jesus Christ. The Eucharist is itself a mystery but not a self-contained mystery. It is the celebration of *the* Christian mystery, communion with God among men, established in and through the death, resurrection, and ascension of Jesus, embracing every generation of mankind ever since, growing toward its ultimate fulfillment when everything in the heavens and earth will be brought together under Christ. This is a mystery so stunning, so overwhelming that its contemplation by the church in the Easter liturgy

prompts the ecstatic cry *O felix culpa,* a truly awesome reaction when one even begins to consider what that *felix
culpa* has led to over the centuries.

Still the mystery has to be preached, pondered, and ap-
propriated by faith before it can be celebrated. There must
be church, people who have allowed themselves to be caught
up in the mystery and sealed by baptism, before there can
be Eucharist. This is a truth, I think, that was widely over-
looked in the excitement over "the changes" that followed in
the wake of Vatican II when we felt the new model mass
would vastly outperform the old in creating "community,"
generating apostles, even reclaiming the disaffected. Somewhat more soberly, we seem to be concerned at the present
with liturgy committees, presidential style, homogeneous
groupings and other strategies we hope will make the mass
work. These and similar efforts are not only appropriate but
desperately important because mechanical, trivialized, life-
less liturgy may not only disappoint or even offend people,
it can erode faith. This, I feel, is precisely what most of the
increasing number of Catholics who "shop around" on Sunday morning have sensed and wish to avoid. Just the same,
mounting meaningful weekend liturgy requires more than
time, artistic creativity, and in large parishes especially,
something that might be called "production expertise." It
means clearly understanding liturgy as a species of common
human activity called ritual that is by no means confined to
the Catholic church, or churches in general for that matter.
Familiarity with the growing body of literature on that sub-
ject would considerably broaden our perspective on the
liturgy and it could help us avoid a multitude of evils in its
making. More than that, it would lead us to focus attention

on two questions that are now, more than ever, of absolutely fundamental importance: what are we actually celebrating on Sunday morning and why? This is to assert that the scope and strength of our faith must occupy us at least as much as the shape of its celebration. Why this is so is the argument of the present chapter.

Man has always been ambivalent about communion with God ever since his primordial sin shattered the original situation in which, Genesis says, he walked with God. Death and the experience of God's absence have haunted him ever since, the dreadful consequences of his self-defeating attempt to be like God, a god himself, separate but equal. Though he has learned long since it is not good for him to be alone, he tries still. And sins. What this means, contemporary theologians have pointed out, is not just formal disobedience of the Great Commandment but a dehumanizing of himself. He clings to the illusion of being a self-made divinity. Sin's terrible irony is seen in the revelation through Christ that humanity is, in Rahner's evocative phrase, "self-alienated divinity."

The church has not always done its best to reduce that ambivalence. For one thing, until recently its proclamation of communion with God achieved by the death of Christ, actualized by the Spirit in the present, toward the supreme moment when he would come again, did not come through as unequivocal "good news." To begin with, the fierce preaching and not a few of the prayers and devotions associated with Lent and Holy Week unfortunately might have led us to sense that there was something unsavory about the way our salvation was won. The unremitting, rhetorically superb emphasis on all the gruesome details of Jesus' "bitter passion" could evoke the deepest feelings of compassion but at the same time seemed to insinuate that God had to have all that blood before agreeing to take us back. After such portrayals we arrived at Easter with both a fresh conviction of the enormity of our sins and a faint but unsettling doubt about the certainty of the Father's benevolence. Perhaps this was why we thought more about the particular judgment than the Parousia and tended in the existential order to conceive salvation as avoiding hell rather than going to heaven. Besides, with all our temporal punishment to be taken care of, heaven did not appear as the likely immediate assignment. We aimed at Purgatory: a miss was as good as a mile. In this crude eschatology of yesteryear, moreover, God was, more than anything else, the implacable judge whose memory was perfect. Heaven meant enjoyment of the beatific vision, a phrase which was theologically precise but not compelling. (What else do you do in heaven besides *see* God?) To be damned entailed the loss of God; but what really bothered us was the thought of an *eternity* of torture and separation from friends and family. We did, of course, value the experience of God we often found in church. It gave us a sense of peace, some assurance that God was on our side, and a deepened conviction that what the catechism said was true. It helped, but we knew very well the one thing necessary was to have sanctifying grace on your soul when you died. It could be lost in a moment. For a Catholic, one White Castle hamburger[2] on Friday (with sufficient reflection and full consent of the will) would do it. Grace was that kind of a thing. God was that kind of friend.

By and large, we have disavowed this caricature of the mystery. From pulpits, in classrooms, in books and articles without number has come the happy news that "God is Love and that he who abides in love abides in God." Yet this authentic revelation has not escaped distortions. Indeed, God loves the people, and in Christ comes as servant. But he comes as the "Suffering Servant" not to do our will but his Father's. His Resurrection uncovered the incredible potential of graced humanity but his death was the quintessential expression of his saving love. At that moment, in that definitive gesture, the "new Adam, the firstborn of men" before the Father and for the people accepted his humanity and ours. What we have sometimes forgotten in the recent recovery of the significance of the resurrection is that we are an "Easter People" only to the extent that we commit ourselves to proclaim the death of the Lord. Love is certainly enough—unless love is thought to be possible without death.

If since Vatican II the church has regained a more biblical outlook and begun to preach the Mystery with greater clarity and emphasis, there is still the matter of practice. Regrettably, the church is often viewed even by many of its own members as failing to practice what it preaches. Writes Charles Meyer:

> [The church] often responds to the challenge of change not at all like a creedal community of hope and love, but after the fashion of a worldly organization, a state, by seeking security in those methods which have worked in the past: by enacting new laws or setting up new punishments—by repressing change with a show of fear rather than encouraging it in hope. It often refuses to take the risk of trusting that the doctrine committed to it by Christ will be understood by men or will be able to inspire them. It holds fast to the doctrine of the Spirit, but puts more reliance in purely human devices. . . . It violates its own principles.[3]

The fact is that it is no longer enough for the church to claim divine authority. Its faith must be transparent. It must offer people, first of all its own faithful, the experience of God in its life, and word, and liturgy, a God in the center of the world to call them to be not less but more deeply human.

Why this is true may not always be obvious. For many Catholics, even those who welcomed the new liturgy *en toto*, all too often there seems to be something, or rather someone, missing. They may speak nostalgically about Latin or complain about the loss of "reverence" but what is meant, whatever reason is adduced, is that they do not have a very satisfying experience of God on Sunday morning. In part, this is due to flaws in the liturgy itself and the way it is celebrated. Beyond that, there is a sense of disillusionment with the church, especially its leaders, who have been found out to be less than divine. The feeling, it strikes me, is very much like that of the adolescent who had learned that his dad is not the smartest nor most powerful man in the world. In many ways the first experience may be more poignant and painful. At any rate, the initial reaction to this discovery seems similar; not unalloyed happiness in one's new "freedom" or dignity but, in the case of the average Catholic, resentment at having been let down, confusion, and hesitation about attributing credibility to anything the church says.

To contend that the church must celebrate more prayerfully and exercise its authority more appropriately is not to say enough. What matters at least as much is the kind of God the church upholds to believers and unbelievers alike. Let us explore this somewhat further.

Western man has from the beginning, as Huston Smith has pointed out, taken seriously the biblical injunction to subdue the earth. He has discovered its secrets and made life less threatening and more comfortable. To put it mildly, until recently he has not been overly concerned with the equitable distribution of the fruits of his developing science and technology. As Saul Bellow reminds us in *Mr. Sammler's Planet,* "It has only been in the last two centuries that the majority of people in civilized countries have claimed the privilege of being individuals. Formerly, they were slave, peasant, laborer, even artisan, but not person."[4] However, this vast scientific and philosophical enterprise that has characterized Western civilization has not always been praised by the church which tended to view each significant scientific advance as a threat to God's sovereignty and, of course, its own. Galileo, Darwin, Freud, to name a few, were, initially at least, blasted, not blessed, by the church. In the long run, at least, this strategy has not enhanced its credibility. It might have been different had the church led the cheers and offered praise and thanksgiving for newly discovered marvels of God all along.

The preoccupation of the church for centuries with the kingdom to come and its tenuous outpost in this life, the supernatural, have had disastrous results which Vatican II could only begin to reverse. Ten years ago, to put it simply, God seemed superfluous. With science and technology and their mighty tool, the computer, man could do it all by himself. Who needed God anyway? A number of Reformed theologians obligingly offered a death notice.

Devoted to the church and generally unafflicted by affluence, Catholics did not interpret their experience in such a way as to reach the same conclusion. God was real enough in the serene certitude and omni-presence of church authority, in the multitude of devotional and not so devotional customs and practices, and especially in the Blessed Sacrament. So too was the prospect of facing him as Judge after this "vale of tears." But when Catholics emerged from the ark, so to speak, after Vatican II, not a few initially hailed the world as paradise found. God was everywhere (except perhaps in church) and all you had to do was "move free," "do your own thing," and "love, love, love." All this is true enough, of course, provided one remembers that the former is the ground of the possibility of the latter. Moreover, in the Christian conception of things the latter is not a fact but a task, or better, man's divinely assigned vocation whose inevitable dynamic was clearly illustrated by the death of Jesus. The Christian mystery does indeed proclaim the world is charged with the grandeur of God. But in the acceptable hyperbole of Brian Wicker, "it must become the purpose of the church in society to make that obvious."

All this is to argue that in our day and age, as far as liturgy is concerned, the message is as important as the medium; in fact, it transcends the medium. Christian liturgy celebrates not just a promise but a presence; not just a kingdom to come but a kingdom that has come in Jesus Christ whose Spirit sent forth into the world at Pentecost guarantees his continued presence there to transform the world fully into his kingdom. Let the proclamation of the mystery and its nuanced affirmation of communion with God past, present, and future get out of phase and the reality of God, or at least the God of Jesus Christ, disappears. For most people in the west, the world is too much with us to find real a God who lies only in the past and the future. Yet to restrict him to the present leads ultimately to the same conclusion. Liturgy ultimately is only as real as the God it celebrates.

That is why, as has been suggested all along, the decisive factors are the strength and scope of faith. Which is to say what a modern Catholic believes about God will determine his approach to the Eucharist. The latter makes sense, glorious sense, only in the context of the gospel of Jesus of Nazareth.

What has come to the fore very recently is the universal need for a gospel, or perhaps more accurately, a faith, a religion. This is not to say, obviously, that everyone wants a supernatural, i.e., a revealed religion. It means simply that a human being must have a reason for living, not an abstract principle, but a deeply personal conviction about the value of reality as a whole that bathes his experience of being in the world with significance. The answer one gives to Alfie's famous question "What's it all about?" is one's religion, or, more simply, one's God; sociologists and anthropologists call it a "meaning system," and understand by the phrase that which an individual finds most real, or "really real," engages his total commitment and determines his perception of what is right and wrong. It could be a career, wealth, science, technology, a cause, an ideology, sport, sex, even one's belly, as St. Paul warned. For those who live by the Judeo-Christian tradition, it is Yahweh-God.

Meaning in this sense, however, arises not from grappling with life's problems but from the experience of its mysteries. Feeding man properly is a problem; why he exists at all is a mystery. To problems we give answers; to mysteries, meaning. The former is a rational operation; the latter involves a total personal response. What this means is that religion is existential in nature. Thus, Christianity or Judaism is not in this primary sense a system of ideas or doctrines about God, but the acceptance of a concrete relationship with him. Religion is not, therefore, knowing about God but the experience of communion with him.

The Judeo-Christian Scriptures explain why, even though God is everywhere in the world, men do not have a constant experience of his presence. Sin destroyed that capacity and made us a people that walk in darkness. Even though Jesus of Nazareth affirmed his continuing presence as the way to the Father, very few of his followers down through the ages have lived with a constant sense of his presence, in what spiritual writers have called "the unitive way." Most of us are limited, or perhaps more accurately, limit ourselves to more sporadic religious experience. We may have so called "peak experiences" of less or greater intensity: a particularly splendid sunset, a violent storm over an ocean, the company of mountains, or an unexpected, dramatic interpersonal experience. But the ordinary place where men have found communion with God is religious ritual.

This may come as a surprise to Catholics who till recently assumed that their liturgy was the absolutely original bequest of Jesus to his church (which the Protestants largely abandoned) and which had nothing at all in common with pagan rites, say, the human sacrifices of the Aztecs, pictures of which they might have seen in the *National Geographic*. The truth is that ritual behavior is a normal human phenomenon. It is the ordinary and indispensable activity men engage in to experience and thereby deepen their relationship not only with God but with each other. Take, for example, the familiar rite of college commencement. It is a splendid illustration of human liturgy, a carefully orchestrated sequence of symbolic actions, meant to renew the commitment of its participants to their Alma Mater. An assembly is called: the graduates, their family and friends, along with the whole hierarchy of the college from the president down to the least assistant professor. If possible a significant place for the ritual is selected, the chapel, the meadow. Vestments are worn which not only distinguish the various ranks within the college but serve to symbolize the unique achievement and worth of its members as opposed to those outside. The rite begins with a solemn procession, the word is proclaimed by some notable from a distant academic institution, then amid the joy, tears, and applause of the entire congregation the college proudly presents a new generation of B.A.'s who come forth single file to receive their birth certificate. Finally the Alma Mater is sung and this elaborate rite of passage ends.

Obviously, commencement isn't absolutely necessary. The time and expense could be saved. Graduates could receive their diplomas by mail with their grades. But the commencement rite offers the opportunity for all who are someway involved in that community to celebrate what they are and what they do. Each symbolic element from the solemn entrance to the singing of the Alma Mater allows meanings to be shared: it was good to be a student; what I have done is valuable; despite my ambiguous feelings, it was good for me to be here.

Of course, when central meanings are not shared, the symbols are abandoned or resisted. A few years ago when campuses were in an uproar; commencement exercises were often disrupted. No wonder, many students at that time simply did not identify with the school and what they felt it stood for. They wanted nothing less than a celebration of their identity with the institution. Their symbolic dress, blue jeans and fatigue jackets instead of caps and gowns, expressed their disaffection and alienation from the community.

Ritual, therefore, is neither peripheral nor, as we once thought in regard to religious ritual, primitive human activity. It is an action or sequence of meaning-filled actions that bolster the unity of people who share those meanings at least to some degree. It may include words, like commencement exercises, or it may be a simple gesture, like a kiss between lovers. The very least rituals do, as social scientists have observed, is make human society possible. This relatively recent insight helps us to understand why men have engaged in religious rites from the earliest times. Symbolic action narrowed the distance between the deity and themselves. It gave them a sense of his presence and assured them that he was on their side and that he would bless their crops and their wars. Christian rites intimate a good deal more, but they do not totally dispel the obscurity, not only because of our ambivalence but also because God is mysterious and so are his actions which the rites are conceived to be.

The latter point is uncommonly important. Louis Bouyer describes a religious rite as a "spontaneous and original manifestation of religion . . . an immediate, primordial creation for religious-minded men in which they have actively realized their effective connection with the divinity before they explain this connection to themselves." And, he adds, "This is why at all times and in all places rites are considered to be the works of the gods. When men find out rites are the work of men, they forget them."[5] Primitive man sensed the sacred in experiences which modern man has for a long time taken for granted: birth, death, harvest, meals, washing, love, marriage. For him these were important moments of life because he was doing what the gods had done. Only later, with the development of a sense of his autonomy, did the simple rites associated with these supreme moments undergo notable elaboration and differentiation. Even then the natural religious symbolism of the rites was not lost sight of, at least not at first.

Catholics have always believed, of course, that the sacraments were instituted by Christ and that he is at work in them. More recently, the parallelism of the sacraments with various events in our ordinary life has been pointed out. I would venture the latter instruction has not done very much to enhance our experience of the sacraments precisely because the religious significance of these human events has generally been obscured if not totally obliterated not so much by the church's emphasis on the supernatural as much as the narrowly rationalist approach to reality that still dominates our age. Granted the birth of a child may still be a religious experience for most parents. It is easy to wonder in the presence of a tiny new creature with ten perfectly formed little fingers: a person! How did it come about? Why? Still, in the contemporary world birth is a statistic, a fact, a problem. How can birth be made less hazardous for mother and child? How can birth be prevented? What is a desirable national birth rate? Or, take nutrition. Again we tend to focus on the problems, biological, social, political. Why are food prices so high? What can I eat and still lose weight? How do we provide hot lunches for slum children? Should we sell wheat to communist countries? I am certainly not suggesting that these and related questions are not valid concerns, problems that can and should be solved or at least alleviated. What has happened, however, is that our more or less general preoccupation with problems in these significant areas of human experience has very largely diminished our awareness of them as mysteries. Problems challenge us and stir us into activity—research and development. Mysteries absorb us and evoke wonder and awe, religious emotions. We solve problems, we celebrate mysteries. Which is to suggest that if we no longer experience his presence so clearly in the Christian mysteries that are the sacraments, at least part of the reason might be that we are not alive to his presence in the human experiences whose deeper meaning they illuminate and transform.

Chapter 4

CELEBRATION OF HIS PRESENCE

. . . I have arisen and am still with you. . . .
                                                    Ps. 138

PROBABLY the most frequently quoted section of Vatican II's *Constitution on the Sacred Liturgy* is paragraph seven, which asserts the multiple presence of Christ in the church: in the Word proclaimed, in the person of the minister of the sacraments and in their saving power, in the liturgical assembly, and especially in the eucharistic species. At least one Catholic theologian hails it as the most important statement of this superb document. Yet some council fathers protested this passage as "novel doctrine" until it was pointed out to them that Pius XII had said substantially the same thing a few years earlier in the encyclical *Mediator Dei.* If the idea seemed new a decade ago to a number of bishops, it was not exactly familiar to the average Catholic either; nor probably has its profound significance been generally appreciated to date. The truth is that we have always believed firmly and rightly gloried in the eucharistic presence of Christ but over the centuries this belief, so rich and full as it came out of the New Testament era, gradually narrowed in focus to the presence of Christ in the sacramental species. Admittedly, this exquisite presence is the distinctive and most awesome element of the mystery that is the Eucharist. However, preoccupation with the raw fact of his presence in the consecrated bread and wine tends to disfigure the meaning of that presence. In effect, it delivers God to us rather than the other way around.

Quite simply, God means to transform us in Christ; that is what the Christian mystery is all about. This mysterious work begun in baptism continues, not exclusively but most fruitfully, in the Eucharist. It is mystery but not magic. It is eloquently described in the Scriptures as a labor of love. God initiates the relationship, man responds. But there is more to the latter than the lighthearted proclamation of one current bumper sticker: "Christ is a Nice Day." Love follows self-disclosure. Christians call God's self-disclosure Revelation. The latter is not, as we are beginning to realize, the communication to man of a set of doctrines and directions, but the act of God's unveiling of himself to us. It is action, Joseph Fitzer aptly says, "specifically, God's act of being present to us in a new way, in Christ, in the Christian mystery." In the Eucharist his presence is real, personal, rich, sacramental. It is loving, forgiving, and comforting. It prompts us to rejoice and repent. This presence of Christ is signified by the consecrated bread and wine but it is specified by the full sacramental event, word and action. In short, the Eucharist tells not only that Christ is present but who it is that we call Christ.

For a long time the church has had a tenuous hold on this basic truth. Canon Law characterized liturgy as the *cultus publicus*, a tidy but barren designation that suggests an extrinsic interpretation of the relation between worship and sanctification. The same tradition held true until recently in textbooks of theology where the worship aspects of the sacraments were dealt with in morality under justice while the grace they produced was discussed under the heading of dogma. What this bifurcation missed was the revelatory character of the liturgy. As long as it lasted, it tended to support the popular notion that mass was a service you were obliged to do for God who came down to listen to your problems and dispense grace and special earthly favors. Its paradigm was more a contract than a covenant. It rendered worship one-sided and, as the Scriptures evidence again and again, easily corruptible, a "bribe" by people "whose hearts," the Lord says, "are far from me."

This is not simply to develop the truth advanced earlier that there must be church to celebrate Eucharist, a people who take their baptismal commitment seriously and who are prepared to worship "in spirit and truth." It is to emphasize, in the words of Gabriel Moran, that "the sacrament is a bright flash in the mystery of revelation now taking place." The Eucharist is a loving encounter with Christ, living and really present, through which we come to know the Father's love and are transformed—graced—by that experience. It is his gift, his love, his word, however, before it is ours. In more traditional language, the sacraments are of Christ's institution, not ours. That is why, if we wish to find the Father of Our Lord Jesus Christ and not a god of our own making, it is necessary to keep in mind all that Jesus did and said at that supper he took with his apostles on the night before he died.

What is to be remembered first is that in response to a query of his disciples, Jesus sent Peter and John to make the preparations for them to eat the Passover. Whether or not the last supper was technically a Passover meal, a fact that the Synoptics affirm but John's chronology seems to disallow, is disputed; but most, though not all scholars, feel that at least it was clearly regarded as such by Jesus and his disciples. Whether or not such was the understanding of Jesus and the disciples, what is not to be forgotten is that it was a *supper*. Until recently, the church had effectively forgotten that. But it is doubtful, I think, that the incessant references to the Eucharist as a meal in the new mass prayers, commentaries, and catechisms have been overly effective, partly because the mass as it is celebrated in most churches still doesn't look very much like a meal, and partly because in our age a meal doesn't mean what it used to. The latter point was raised earlier, but it deserves further development. It is indicative of the unhappy fact that in a busy, restless, preoccupied technological society we have largely diminished our capacity to celebrate anything.

Primitive man, as Mircea Eliade has shown, did not take his daily bread for granted, not because he was worried about where the next meal was coming from, but because he felt nourishment was something sacred. It reunited him with the creative power of the cosmos. It was a holy, sanctifying action even before he made it a sacrament. That is why the sacred meal, whether it was conceived as feeding the gods or eating with them or simply in their presence, has been viewed as a privileged *means of communion*. And whatever its specific occasion, deity was adored, implored, and thanked in this seemingly ordinary human gesture, that of itself professed man's utter dependence on God and his need for communion with the source of his life.

For the ancient semitic peoples, sacred meals possessed a significance of which only a small residue still remains.

Those who ate together felt committed to one another. Violation of this covenant was akin to sacrilege. Thus the Psalmist's bitter lament: "Even my closest and most trusted friend, *who shared my table*, rebels against me" (Ps. 41:9). A meal thus had a religious significance that had clear social consequences.

The Hebrew religion recognized this natural religious symbolism but it made a decisive and creative change in the meaning of various pagan ritual meals. Whatever the specific mythic images that developed around them, pagan rites represented people searching for God. In Israel it was exactly the other way around: God revealed himself and chose a people. It was Yahweh who brought the Jews out of Egypt, guided and watched over them in the wilderness, and made a covenant with them on Sinai. It was Yahweh who led them into the land of Canaan where he prepared a table for them in the midst of their enemies. It was Yahweh who punished their infidelity and yet promised them a Messiah who would institute in his blood a new and everlasting covenant. It was Yahweh who fashioned their history and gave them rituals to celebrate his enduring love for them.

The Jews felt their rites were divinely revealed, though their concrete forms underwent considerable development over the centuries. This evolution is perhaps best understood as a gradual refining, under the influence of a deepening faith, of cultic practices of pre-Mosaic origin and rites borrowed from neighboring pagan tribes. The Passover is a good case in point. The Jewish festival par excellence, it celebrates the central events that have always dominated Jewish consciousness, Exodus and the Sinai covenant. Yet contemporary scholars have discovered the existence of a passover celebration among nomadic shepherds. Its occasion was the beginning of spring pasture and it entailed the sacrifice of a young animal whose blood was sprinkled on the tent-poles to secure the well-being of the tribe. Exodus 12:11 suggests a modification of an existing rite rather than the introduction of something altogether new when it explains, "It is a passover *in honor of Yahweh.*"[1] Well before the time of Christ the Jewish Passover also was fused with another ancient rite of spring that originated with agricultural peoples, the Feast of the Unleavened Bread. During the biblical period there were some variations in the shape of the celebration; and what began as a predominately family celebration gradually assumed a wider significance as a renewal of the bond that linked the entire Jewish people. Nonetheless, late descriptions of the Passover yield a rite that is substantially the same as that of Exodus 12, the distinctive features of which the eating of the Paschal lamb, unleavened bread, bitter herbs, and the Passover *haggadah* recited by the Father or head of the group, have become better known to Catholics in recent years. Its annual celebration was not a simple recalling of what Yahweh had done for them "in the old days," so to speak, but came through the eschatological thrust of the prophets to be a vivid expression of their conviction that he stood with them still and that at the appointed time would bring about a glorious tomorrow, Exodus fulfilled. Their eating the Passover meal, however, was not only expressive of their hope in Yahweh who had made a covenant with them; it offered them an experience of his presence, a foretaste of that future Passover, their tradition said, when the Messiah would come to establish once and for all the reign of Yahweh. Not surprisingly, the image of that supreme event was a banquet.

The same Jewish hopes were kept alive through the less elaborate Sabbath meal observed by devout families and rabbis and their followers. Bread was blessed and broken and eaten by all present, who also shared a ceremonial cup of wine. These gestures were accompanied by a rather extended prayer of thanksgiving and praise (*berakah*) for God's mighty works on their behalf in the past and in the future. Undoubtedly, Jesus kept this custom of eating the Sabbath meal with his disciples. The meal they had on the night before he died was, indeed, the *last* supper.

In a much greater sense, it was the first. What men from the beginning had sought and sensed obscurely in the ordinary action of eating together, what they had tried in vain to effect in various kinds of ritual meals, what the Jews had hoped for in their covenant meals, especially the Paschal meal, was now a reality. God had come in Jesus to establish communion with men. The deeper significance of human meals was validated. "The good news implicit in the Eucharist," says Gregory Baum, "is that God offers men redemption through common meals."

The New Testament offers four accounts of the extraordinary words and actions of Jesus at that supper the night before his death: Mt. 26:26–29; Mk. 14:22–25; Luke 22:15–20; and I Cor. 11:23–25. Written much later, John's Gospel records other details of the meal and some beautiful words that Jesus may very well have spoken to the disciples on that occasion but it does not mention the Eucharist, though its sixth chapter gives a clear promise (John 6:53–58). The four institution narratives are obviously liturgical formulas which apparently represent two somewhat different traditions, one common in Palestinian communities (Mark), the other from

Hellenistic churches (Paul). While the words differ in all four versions they are in substantial accord and attention to the actions of Jesus reveals their significance.

Following the custom at such meals, at the beginning of the main course, Jesus took bread, blessed it, broke it, then shared it with his friends. Normally, this was a simple gesture that meant everyone at the table shared the favor of the head of the house. Usually it was enhanced by silence while the bread went around. On this night the silence was broken by the awesome words: "This is my body, which is for you" (I Cor. 11:25–26). Normally, the father or host passed his own cup only to an honored guest as a sign of his special honor and affection. At the Last Supper all the apostles received the cup of Jesus.

What emerges from this is a realization of the awesome significance of what Jesus did. He announced that in him the history of the world had come to its decisive turning point. His death would accomplish what all liturgy, pagan as well as Jewish, had tried but could never effect, reconciliation with God. His body would be broken for them; his blood would be poured out to embrace them and establish a new and everlasting covenant that Jeremiah had promised long ago. It was the Christian mystery preached during his public life, proclaimed now through an ancient ritual whose meaning and power, that is to say its reality, he profoundly transformed. If God has fed his people with manna in the desert and milk and honey in the land of Canaan, his gift now was the flesh of the Son of Man. If previously the drinking of the blood of animals was forbidden because blood was a unique symbol of life and thus belonged to God himself, now he offered his son's blood. If the first covenant had been sealed by Moses' sprinkling of the people with blood, the new covenant was sealed by the drinking of that son's blood. Thus Paul exclaims: "The blessing-cup that we bless is a communion with the blood of Christ, and the bread that we break is a communion with the body of Christ" (I Cor. 10:16).

That the apostles obeyed the command of Jesus to do what he had done at the Last Supper in his memory is clear from the New Testament. That their joy, even euphoria, was the direct result of their conviction that he was present in their midst is also a matter of record. That some of their followers very early began to misinterpret the meaning of his presence, however, is also, unfortunately, true. Yet, it compelled Paul, under the influence of the Spirit, to develop that meaning even more clearly for the church. If baptism meant incorporation in the death of Jesus, Eucharist was a continuing proclamation of that death. For Paul that death was the divine instrument for striking down all barriers that separated God from men and men from each other. The two projects were inseparable. Christ's presence in the world was to accomplish both. "He is the peace between us," writes Paul in the letter to the Ephesians, and "through him, both of us have in the one Spirit our way to come to the Father."

This dynamic and integral notion of Christ's presence in the Eucharist lasted for a long time. What mattered most for the early Christians was not how he was there nor even simply that he was there, but what he was doing there, or better, what he was doing in them. It was truly his body and blood they received but it was his *given* body and *shed* blood, which offered them freedom from sin, and bound them to him in a new covenant unity. John's Gospel emphasized the Eucharist as eschatological food; but, as the

Protestant scholar Oscar Cullman pointed out in recent years, the frequent sacramental allusions in his gospel were meant precisely to link the saving action of Jesus' public life with what he continued to do in the life of the church. Ignatius called the Eucharist the "medicine of immortality" and the "antidote against death" but these were not static images. None of this prompted a casual attitude toward the Eucharistic species. In the first century Justin stressed the difference between Eucharist and ordinary bread and other Fathers called for the utmost reverence in handling the consecrated species. Thus, the *Mystagogic Catecheses* of Jerusalem instructed the faithful about receiving Communion:

> When you approach, do not go stretching out your open hands or having your fingers spread out, but make the left hand into a throne for the right which shall receive the King, and then cup your open hand and take the Body of Christ, reciting the *Amen*. Then sanctify with all care your eyes by touching the Sacred Body, and receive it.[2]

Even this simple pastoral instruction is a delicate emphasis on the personal presence of Christ. Reverence is prescribed precisely because what one receives is the body of Christ, the King.

It should be remembered though that the early church lived in a Platonic world which thought of material reality as a faint shadow of the authentic world which was spiritual. (The action, so to speak, was in the latter.) It thrived on symbolism and tended to find in both cosmic and human events profuse evidence of the power of the divine and demonic. In this atmosphere it was perhaps easier to accept the active personal presence of Christ in the Eucharist. It certainly did not seem necessary to try and explain it.

That did seem necessary to Thomas Aquinas a few centuries ago. Reacting to the Eucharistic controversies that had begun toward the end of the so-called Dark Ages, he emphasized the spiritual presence of the Lord's Body; and in an age that thrilled to stories of bleeding hosts and white wine turning red, he taught that Christ was really present not alongside, beyond, or beside but in the sign. Even so, he did not do so calmly but felt compelled to add later: "I refer to the judgment of the Holy Roman Church everything that I have taught or written about the sacrament of the body of Christ and the other sacraments."

Against Lutheran denials the Council of Trent affirmed the real sacramental presence and the change of bread and wine into the body and blood of Christ which this presence demands. The expression that "most fittingly" describes this change said the Council Fathers, good Aristotelians that they were, was "transubstantiation," a word that later became dear to the heart of every Catholic school child.

If Trent happily insisted on the objective reality of Christ's presence in the Eucharist, it did not promote with equal energy a robust sacramentalism in its theology or liturgy that could have interdicted the common view of the Eucharist as a sacred thing. During the Middle Ages that was precisely what sacrament came to mean, whereas it had formerly enjoyed the much wider meaning of its Greek equivalent *mysterion* which signified first of all an action, a representation of an event. That understanding of sacrament continued down to our own day. A sacrament was a holy thing to be received. To be sure, in the Eucharist Christ was really present but he had nothing to say, or rather, people no longer understood his language.

The latter point requires explanation. Liturgy is language, a set of symbols, verbal ("This is my Body") and non-verbal (bread and wine). The value of language is that it mediates personal presence. It is self-disclosure, self-revelation, the way persons get in touch with each other. It deals with meanings, which are what constitute the distinctly human world. Now the church has always believed that it got its liturgy from Jesus Christ. It has also always held fast to the belief that whenever it performed the liturgy, through the power of the Holy Spirit Christ was present, especially in the sacrament of the Eucharist. But what it forgot for a long time was that the liturgy is language, Christ's living word to us which, through the same Holy Spirit, is heard, and believed, and thus becomes our word. When that was not understood it didn't really matter that mass was in Latin, that it could never have been confused with a fraternal meal, and that people did not generally participate in it or even know what it meant. What did matter was that Jesus was present and we could talk to him. We did not know clearly but at least he was saying something to us.

In a very real sense, the changes in the mass since Vatican II represent an implementation of this insight into liturgy as language. They are meant to make the Eucharist a clear, powerful, infinitely rich language so that his presence might be deeply experienced and effect our salvation. They are based on a newly recovered appreciation of the fact that the ordinary way God communicates with us in the liturgy or elsewhere is through material reality. It is his Spirit that makes us alive to the meaning of that reality.

What helped fashion this outlook on Gods' presence in the world that is so evident especially in the principal documents of Vatican II was mainly but not merely the extraordinary biblical and liturgical scholarship that led up to the Council. It stemmed also from the existentialist and phenomenological philosophies that had begun to offer theologians a cogent, contemporary language for their theology. These philosophies were, and are, concerned with the problem of human meaning. If in a Platonic world things are never what they seem, in the modern world things are precisely what they *mean*. A kiss between lovers is two sets of lips touching. But what does it mean? "I love you." "I'm sorry." "I forgive you." "You're great." That is what it *is*. It is persons being present to each other. Or my typewriter: An extraordinary collage of steel, rubber and felt that prints letters when I touch the keys. For me it is also a source of wonder and pleasure, an old friend, a focus of near endless associations, an indispensable tool that makes written communication possible, a gift. All this and more is what my typewriter *means* to me. The existentialist responds, all this is what it *is*.

In recent years theologians have wondered whether this kind of thinking might help illuminate what the church has always believed about the Eucharist—that ordinary bread and wine becomes the body and blood of Christ. There is no dispute about or denial of the fact of that presence or the change that effects it. The problem is how to explain it. Trent was thinking in Aristotelian categories (the only ones it had) when it said that the substance of the bread and the wine changes while the accidents remain and that the best word around to describe the process was "transubstantiation." However, since modern physics has displaced Aristotelian science, a circumstance which makes "substance" a very slippery notion, modern theology has suggested that "transubstantiation" may no longer be the very best word to explain Eucharistic presence. Much better words might be

"transignification" (change in signification) or "transfinalization" (change in purpose). Ordinary bread and wine become
the body and blood of Christ given to us in the Eucharist
because through the power of the Holy Spirit Christ changes
their meaning. This change of meaning, which only he could
bring about, yields his real, personal, saving presence.

In a sense, the current controversy about the Eucharist
is over which comes first, new reality or new meaning. Everyone admits that the Eucharist involves both. A few years ago
after an uproar in Holland caused by some well-meant but
misleading theological talk about the Real Presence which
Time magazine further mangled in its report, Pope Paul
hurried to explain in *Mysterium Fidei* that there was, indeed,
transignification and transfinalization in the Eucharist but
only because there was transubstantiation. In other words,
new reality causes new meaning. Behind this assertion is the
view that meaning is a psychic rather than an ontologic reality, that is, meaning is only in the mind not a full, inde-
pendent, extramental reality. Many theologians continue to
think that just the contrary is true and that their approach
has more support from the Bible and the Fathers of the
church. This complex inquiry proceeds; but it is important
for us non-theologians to realize that both sides are united
in a common faith in the reality of that Presence and both
would wholeheartedly echo the well-known prayer of Teil-
hard de Chardin:

> O Lord! Grant that your descent beneath the universal
> species be not cherished and caressed as the fruit of philo-
> sophical speculation but that it may become for me truly a
> real presence! By power and right, whether we will it or
> not, you are incarnate in the world and we live caught up
> in you!

Chapter 5

RENEWAL OF COMMITMENT

. . . This was to create one single New Man in himself out of the two of them and by restoring peace through the cross, to unite them both in a single Body and reconcile them with God.

Eph. 2:15

I F VATICAN II spirituality had to be characterized in a phrase, surely a top entry would have to be, "They shall know we are Christians by our love." That theme has been preached (wisely, but not always well), prayed, even danced but perhaps not generally believed. In fact, most of us would reluctantly admit that our performance as individuals or as a group would not on that ground establish our Christian identity even for one another. It was easier in the past. We went to mass every Sunday, ate fish on Friday, sent our children to Catholic schools, obeyed the Pope, and never thought of thinking for ourselves at all. (What, never? Well, hardly ever.) We knew who we were and everybody else did too. Our problem now is that "new commandment" of Jesus. It seems at once wonderfully attractive and utterly impossible.

It wasn't meant to be. That is precisely the good news. But perhaps a large part of our difficulty is, and always has been, faint-heartedness; the news is too good to believe, so we water it down. We take all the talk about God's love in the Scriptures as a proposition rather than a promise, as though what God says to us is, "Keep my commandments and *then* I will love you." In other words, good performance earns salvation. That, of course, is often how it works among us, as psychologists have pointed out to parents especially in recent years. But what God has told us, most clearly and completely in Christ, is that he is utterly different: he loves first, last, and always. Where there is love in the world, there is God. And insofar as we open up to that love, let it take possession of us and transfigure us, the New Commandment becomes not only possible but, in a sense, irresistible. More and more we become for each other the "glory of the Lord," and because we have this hope, Paul says, "we are very bold" (II Cor. 3:12).

That is not pious rhetoric, but revelation. It is the mystery which the Eucharist so exquisitely expresses and extends. To Paul we are in debt for the very large hint of an explanation of this mystery. Though we are many, Jew and Gentile, white and black, rich and poor, old and young, we are brought together in Christ. This is not to be taken to mean that the church is simply a voluntary association of like minded men united more or less closely by their belief in Jesus Christ and adherence to his moral teaching. It is infinitely more. We do not merely follow Christ and in some vague way "represent" him in the world, we *become* Christ. "You together are Christ's body," Paul tells us (I Cor. 12:27). But when we hear these words we are tempted to think, "Oh, what a lovely metaphor." That has been the inclination of the church since the second half of the 12th century, deLubac lamented; it was at that point that the body of Christ which is the church itself begins to be qualified by the adjective "mystical." However, modern theologians braced by the enormous scripture scholarship and the new appreciation of the Fathers of the past few decades are not so timid in interpreting Paul. They have located the sources of the latter's realism in his Hebrew anthropology which sees the body as an animated corporeal person and not as a prison for the soul, in his application to Christ of the ancient Jewish notion of corporate personality, and in his insistence that in feeding on the Eucharist the community actually becomes the glorified Body of Christ. What this bold, realistic, relentlessly biblical thinking yields is an ontological rather than a moral ground for our unity as Christians. We are one in the Lord not because of what we do but because of what he does in us. He incorporates us into his resurrected humanity; we become truly the risen body of Christ, "more truly his body" Boussuet said, "than his own body." We are, in short, not a metaphor but a mystery.

All this helps to reveal the depths of meaning in the traditional designation of the Eucharist as the sacrament of unity. The Eucharist is a celebration of, by, and for the Body of Christ. It is body becoming body. We eat and drink to become what we are. Thus, deLubac says:

> It would therefore be wrong to do no more than talk of a "physical" body of Christ present in the Eucharist and then of another body which is "mystical"; merely linking the two more or less closely. That is certainly not how St. Paul saw it. For him, there is only one body of Christ—Christ's resur-

rected humanity. But the church who exists only by participation in this humanity of Christ, the "life-giving Spirit," who is offered to her in the Eucharist, is herself simply the "fullness of him who fulfills himself wholly in all things."[1]

The same idea is developed in at least equally forthright language by Charles Meyer in his *A Contemporary Theology of Grace:*

> The words of the priest: "This is my body; this is my blood" are pronounced primarily over the congregation and only in a secondary sense over the gifts which represent the people present. It is only because the church, a segment of which they are, actually constitutes the body of Christ, and because Christ is personally present in his church, of which the priest is the official spokesman, that what they are can become sacramentally present under the appearances of bread and wine. Thus the identity between Christ and Christians initially expressed at baptism is proclaimed again at Mass.[2]

But perhaps no one has matched the limpid beauty of St. Augustine's testimony of this ultimate truth about the Eucharist:

> It is your very own mystery which is laid upon the Lord's table; it is your mystery which you receive; you reply "Amen" to the affirmation of what you are yourself.

Compelling affirmations about the Eucharist such as these may lead one to conclude that Christianity is an incomparably beautiful religion, which it is, and incredibly painless, which it is not. That was exactly the error of the Corinthians, a perennial one, it should be admitted, very much alive at the present time: instant salvation, Christianity without the cross.

I think that the real problem is, in Augustine's words, to "reply 'Amen,'" not just from one's lips, of course, but from the depths of one's grace-won freedom. For Christians that word of living faith is addressed precisely to the reality of the Body of Christ, to all that Body is together with all that is not yet but is to become. It is first spoken at Baptism. Thereafter, it cannot be confined to the moment of Eucharist but there it assumes its most tangible, eloquent, and efficacious expression. There too it appears most clearly as a surrender to that reality's inexorable demand, which is nothing less than our glad and grateful commitment to die with Christ. The Eucharist is the sacramental renewal of that commitment. It is for that reason called the "sacrifice of the church."

We have had our problems with that idea. From our childhood on we were taught that the mass was a *sacrifice;* but in order to explain what that meant our teachers almost invariably fell back on accounts of what the pagans did to animals (or virgins) in their temples. The animals were slaughtered which was the only decisive way of removing them from human circulation and thus "giving them" to the god or gods, who were supposed to return this act of obeisance with renewed benevolence. They didn't work for the pagans because they had the wrong god. The Jews did; but all their sacrifices couldn't open the gates of heaven because human sin, even the smallest, was an offense against the infinite dignity of God and could only be atoned for by God himself. God loved us; but he had his principles. However, he sent his only beloved Son into the world to suffer in our place. Just becoming a man would have atoned for all the sins that ever were and ever would be committed, but Jesus willingly underwent suffering and death in order to reveal the fullness of divine love. On Calvary he offered himself to the Father and was crucified. He was both priest and victim. Divine justice was satisfied, divine love revealed, heaven opened. The mass is an unbloody version of Christ's sacrifice on Calvary, which is represented by the separation of species on the altar. It is a true sacrifice, only now through the priest we offer Christ to the Father; or, as it has been restated since the atonement theory lost ground, Christ offers us to the Father.

Now both statements are, in fact, misleading. They are, I think, the result of a long-standing tendency of theologians to define sacrifice in terms of its morphology rather than its meaning or significance and to understress the radical discontinuity between Jewish and pagan sacrifices and the sacrifice of Christ. Over the centuries this reductionist approach to the sacrificial nature of the mass has caused serious distortions. It clericalized the mass, obscured its character as a fraternal meal, and sentimentalized Holy Communion. Sacrifice came to be thought of as something going on at the altar. It laid no specific claim on our hearts.

We have a better idea now. In recent years comparative religion has prompted theologians and liturgists to reappraise the traditional approach to sacrifice and return to the original idea. Careful research has established the fact that while there existed some variation in what men meant, there was considerable diversity in what they did when they were at sacrifice. For instance, sacrifice often entailed the destruction of a victim, but not always; many primitive sacrifices did not involve immolation. Sometimes a meal was included, sometimes not. Frequently, sacrifice was seen as the presentation of the deity with a gift; but this represents a far too sophisticated interpretation of the sacrificial rites of many primitive tribes. The new-found awareness of diversity in sacrificial rites has led contemporary theologians to define sacrifice in terms of its significance rather than attempt to extract some essence out of its multiple forms. Thus Nicholas Lash speaks of sacrifice as "an action whose meaning or purpose is to share divine life by man."[3] In other words, sacrifice is what men do to experience communion with God. It is the technical term for human love addressed to God.

Primitive man, it was remembered earlier, had a pervasive but diffuse notion of the sacred. His simple rituals focused on the ordinary events of life, birth, death, love, eating and drinking, planting and harvesting, in which he was absorbed in the supernatural, repeating what the gods had done. Later, as man's sense of autonomy developed, the presence of the divine was delimited to a mountain, or a forest, or later to a shrine or a temple. At the same time man began to exhibit a strange ambivalence toward the numinous—both fear and fascination. A priesthood evolves to cope with this ambivalence; the gods are to be approached but only by specially designated persons. Sacrifice became more elaborate and sometimes embraced the ritual slaying of an infant or a captured warrior from another tribe. Father Lash thinks that a radical separation of the cult people from the general populace indicates a strong doctrine of vicarious cult activity and a magical attitude toward ritual. That would seem to be a particularly illuminating theory when applied to the Catholic church of yesteryear. Whatever the case, the main point is that pagan man did, indeed, long for the touch of God and his ritual sacrifice should be seen as an expression of that longing. If he did multiply false gods and attempt to manipulate them, that propensity is still observable in contemporary man and must be adjudged, therefore, to be a function of sin as well as ignorance. And if his rites were sometimes gruesome, this may be evidence not just of his barbarity but of the desperate character of his need and the violence of his search.

In Israel there was also a temple, a priesthood, and sacrifice. But Yahweh had spoken through Moses and continued to speak through a long line of prophets; and his Word gave sacrifice a decisive new meaning—fidelity to the covenant. "Only a virtuous man's offering graces the altar, and its savor rises before the Most High" (Sirach 35:5). Without wholehearted commitment to Yahweh sacrifices were empty and deceitful; their smoke was, Yahweh complained, "stench in my nostrils." What pleased Yahweh ultimately was for his people "to let the oppressed go free, and break every yoke, to share your bread with the hungry, and shelter the homeless poor, to clothe the man you see to be naked, and not turn from your own kin" (Isaiah 58:7-8). The severe condemnation of religious formalism by the prophets, however, is not to be taken as wholesale rejection of any ritual sacrifice. The latter was held in high esteem in Israel and throughout the Biblical period it assumed various forms. Though within the context of the Covenant it exhibited a vastly purified understanding of themes that also characterized pagan sacrifice—expiation, recognition of the dominion of God, absolute dependence, and communion with God—Jewish sacrifice also expressed a grateful acknowledgement of Yahweh's goodness in the past and, especially after the exile, the desire and hope for a more perfect union with him in the future.

That union, Christians believe, was established in Jesus Christ. The stupendous fact that the Son of God embodied himself in this world and did not emerge from it makes the very humanity of Jesus sacrificial. But in accepting death Jesus uttered on our behalf a decisive, unconditional, enduring word of love for the Father; and his resurrection followed not, as Karl Rahner has pointed out, as another event after that passion and death, but as the manifestation of what happened in that death. Thus his death-resurrection was the definitive declaration of the love of God for us and his ascension sent forth into the world the Holy Spirit so that this saving declaration might be heard until the end of time and gather all who respond with grateful love into the unimaginable intimacy of the body of Christ.

The earliest Christians believed the end of time had been announced by Jesus who was still with them in the Spirit but would shortly return to gather up all who had heard the word, believed, and were baptized in his name. They were taken up with the wondrous newness and finality of their situation. The old order of always waiting, of hope ending in disappointment, along with everything that went with it—the Law, the temple, the priests, scribes and Pharisees—all that was over. The future had arrived because this Jesus of Nazareth, the great Prophet, the New Moses, had risen from the dead and all that he promised would shortly come true. This conviction was reinforced by the marvels that happened in the community, the speaking in tongues, miraculous healings. They came together to learn more about what Jesus had said and to celebrate the Lord's Supper as he had commanded. But the meaning of his death, which had at first been a source of scandal, they expressed not in explicitly sacrificial terms but in scriptural categories: Christ was the new passover, the Suffering Servant of Deutero-Isaiah who died for the people and thereby inaugurated a new and everlasting covenant in his blood. It was that covenant into which they passed in baptism and which they celebrated in the Lord's Supper.

It may be hard for us who have perhaps only rescued that word from the scriptures since Vatican II and who have for centuries spoken of marriage as a *contract* rather than a covenant (which is what it is) to appreciate the evocative character of that word for the early Christians. Many of them were Jews. More important, their leaders, the Apostles, were Jews—radical Jews, it is usually forgotten—whose lives had been dominated by the covenant and who were drawn to Jesus because of his transparent spirituality. To them he seemed the fulfillment of the covenant, the personification of what Judaism really stood for, the hope for its restoration. His justice exceeded that of the scribes and Pharisees; his authoritative teaching echoed the spirit of Moses and transcended it; his presence radiated the divine more than the temple whose priests had been in disrepute for many years. After his resurrection, they came to realize what he had said to them on the night before he died and what he had accomplished by dying and rising from the dead: The new covenant, prophesied in the distant past by Jeremiah, had been established. This covenant required a spiritual circumcision, belief in the risen Lord Jesus who would return to raise them up and lead them to the Father. This belief in him would eventually result in their being put to death, Jesus had predicted. Nonetheless, filled with the Spirit they gathered with great joy to eat and drink his supper of the new covenant. It was the precious memorial of him that he had given them, the unique expression of their desire to keep faith with him, and the particular moment of realization that he lived now in them and they in him. If they did not at first speak of it as a sacrifice, it was that they were overwhelmed and absorbed by its meaning.

The Epistle to the Hebrews compares the death of Christ to pagan and Jewish sacrifice but the relationship is of archetype to type. In other words, all other sacrifices have to be measured against the sacrifice of Christ and not the other way around. The well known cry of the early Christians "we have no altars or temples" reveals an acute awareness of the emphatic difference in meaning sacrifice assumes with Christ. Before him, sacrifice concretized man's search for God and it revealed even in Israel, and perhaps more dramatically there, man's inability to embrace him. But in the death-resurrection-ascension of Christ sacrifice means God's finding man and drawing man to himself. The church then is nothing but the deployment of that sacrifice; it has no meaning, no existence apart from that event. It is, simply, the people who allow themselves to be found by God in Christ and cling to him. The church ultimately has no gift, no sacrifice, but itself; that is what through the Spirit it remembers, proclaims, becomes when it celebrates the Eucharist. And there it says, "This is my Body" not to have his body present but to be, or better, *become* more fully through the same Spirit his body present. The church has a priesthood but that priesthood is not so much over or apart from the church, but a blessing within the church, the sacrament of its unity and authenticity as being itself, "a chosen race, a royal priesthood, a consecrated nation" (I Pet. 2:9).

This sense of the clear-cut difference between Christ's sacrifice and those of the past lasted more or less intact for centuries even though very early the Fathers began to speak of the Christian ministry in terms of the Old Testament priesthood. However, it did not effectively survive when those persistent comparisons were accentuated by the liturgical decadence that accompanied the wave of exaggerated Chalcedonianism that swept through Europe during the Dark Ages. Still it remained for Peter Lombard at the beginning of the Middle Ages to herald the *unbroken* line between the Aaronic and the New Testament priesthood. And because every Scholastic theologian worth his salt felt obliged to compose variations on the themes of Peter Lombard's famous *Sentences*, his "altar and temple" view of sacrifice and priesthood which was so different from that of early Christian tradition took hold.

It was a disaster. Until twenty years ago Catholic theologians spent a great deal of time *proving* that mass was a sacrifice (largely for the benefit of Protestants). In the process they obscured the character of the mass as a fraternal meal, wrote everyone but the priest out of the sacrifice, and confused its relationship with Calvary. One particularly important step in this development was the consensus that emerged in the 13th century that located the essential form of the mass in the institution narrative. "In this perspective," writes Edward Kilmartin, S.J., "the oblationary language of the prayers followed the words of consecration, e.g., *memores offerimus*, were gradually referred not to the offering which the church makes of herself in union with Christ but to the body and blood of Christ."[4] Thus the common understanding of the mass developed that Christ *came down* at the words of consecration and *then* the priest offered him to the Father. It was Calvary all over again only in an unbloody form. Some went so far as to suggest it was something more.

This was not the view of Thomas Aquinas nor of the Council of Trent; both echoed the original tradition that the mass was a sacrifice in that it was an effective memorial of Christ's death. But Aquinas fudged his position with misleading sacrificial language and Trent failed to get through because it did not integrate what it had to say about the mass as a sacrifice with its theology of the Real Presence. Thus, until recently we thought of the mass as a sacrifice at which we received a sacrament. The former wasn't really any of our business. Sacrifice had been repaganized.

Contemporary theologians have regained the spirit of the Fathers in calling the Eucharist the sacrament of the sacrifice of Christ—a memorial filled with the reality of Christ's sacrifice. What this means is admirably outlined in Father Kilmartin's report on current thinking about the Eucharist.

> (1) Christ is actively present by identity with the action of the priest recalling the words and gestures of Christ by which he revealed his self-offering for the world at the Last Supper. (2) As a result of this active presence of Christ, he becomes substantially present as the "given" person in the Eucharistic species. (3) The Eucharistic words are not only spoken by Christ through the priest, thus causing his sacrifice to be present; they are also spoken by Christ to the church, and so becoming the church's word of faith. As spoken by the church, they proclaim the church's faith in Christ's sacrifice and her desire to be united to it. (4) The Eucharistic presence of Christ is a sign that the church's worship is acceptable to God; and communion of the body and blood of Christ signifies the deeper involvement in the paschal mystery in its personal and social dimensions.[5]

This explanation turns on the biblical notion of anamnesis, the special act of remembrance the church is capable of precisely because it is the Body of Christ. This is effectively different from the kind of remembering we may do of, say, John XXIII. We read his biography and are captivated once again by the words and actions of this saintly, much loved Pope. We may feel very close to him but his presence to us is a matter of subjective recall. When the church remembers Christ's sacrifice by celebrating the Eucharist, we are not, as it were, remembering alone. The church participates in the memory of the Spirit of Christ and thus makes the sacrifice of Christ objectively present. The latter is so present, therefore, because it has become—and in a real sense only insofar as it has become—the sacrifice of the church.

All this should suggest that sacrifice is not only what the church *does* but what the church *is*. The deepest meaning of the word (*sacrum facere*) is to make holy. What is made holy by Christ's sacrifice is a people who become the People of God, the church. Nevertheless, God does not violate our autonomy. His word of love that is Christ requires a free response of faith. That faith, obviously, implies more than assent to a Denziger of doctrines, more than observance of commandments, and certainly more than participation in liturgy. It means total surrender, the purest sort of intention to embrace the pain as well as the joy of becoming human— a vocation whose glory was revealed in Christ and whose possibility is secured by his grace.

But we never quite manage that. We are never fully church, never completely "a living sacrifice of praise." That is why the Eucharist, "that first ecstasy" of grace, as Father Meyer so evocatively describes it, is also a celebration of Christian hope and a renewal of our commitment to a life that gives stunning witness to the truth that God means to be all in all.

Chapter 6

TOMORROW WILL BE BETTER

The liturgy . . . is a human action in which the faith of the community becomes a sign of the action of the living God. If the human action ceases to be a powerful sign, the sacred lies hidden; the faith deteriorates, the religious significance of the action is obscured.

André Laurentin

I T WAS Schillebeeckx, I think, who a few years ago suggested we should not be discouraged by the fact that one out of four married couples gets divorced but rather be astonished that three out of four stay together. His point, of course, was that years ago economic realities, legal sanction, and social pressure made divorce either impossible or uncommonly difficult. It is generally not so any longer. We might marvel, therefore, that most couples stay together, presumably out of love. Probably not everyone will agree either with that interpretation or evaluation of the current status of the institution of marriage but it occurred to me that something similar might be said about the latest statistic of weekly mass attendance among Catholics. We're under 60% now, a drop of over 10 percentage points from a decade ago. But perhaps since many no longer consider weekly mass *de rigeur,* we should rejoice that the majority still does go every Sunday, presumably out of some positive religious motive. I joke not, though it does seem that our majority is increasingly a coalition of the very young and the very old. However, with the absolutely unprecedented upheavals in society as well as the Catholic church compounded by the latter's apparent intention to replicate within a decade, as Jaroslav Pelikan observed, all the mistakes the Protestant churches had made over the last 400 years, the fidelity of the majority to a weekly Eucharist might well be a cause for wonder in the biblical sense of the word. Not lacking, moreover, especially in the past year or two, are other signs that the church may be doing nicely with Future Shock after all, thank you.

The point here though is not to count heads but to analyze our problem somewhat further and to suggest some approaches. The *Constitution on the Sacred Liturgy* says, "The Liturgy is the summit toward which the activity of the church is directed; at the same time it is the fountain from which all her power flows. . . . From the liturgy, therefore, and especially from the Eucharist, as from a fountain, grace is channeled into us." Or, as Gabriel Moran put it, "The Eucharist is the church at her best." But the superlative assumes genuine meaning only when both are experienced as good and holy. There exists a reciprocal relationship between the church and the Eucharist; one can't really be improved without the other.

This has been a favorite theme of Karl Rahner, who has repeatedly stressed the continuity between Christian faith and sacramental action. The latter, he explains, permits faith to grow strong and mature by becoming more intense and tangible in external action. However, writing in the heady climate of the early Sixties when liturgical reform tended to be viewed as a panacea, he emphasized the importance of faith and devotion as indispensable dispositions for the meaningful celebration of the Eucharist. While not short-changing the grace-giving potential of the Eucharist in the slightest, he insisted that "the reception and increase of this same grace can happen and is meant to happen in Christian life itself. We are meant to come back from our lives to the altar full of the grace given to us through those lives, because it is only thus, coming from life to the altar, that we are able and worthy to do what must be done there."[1] Rahner's perfectly balanced statement is fully in accord with Thomas Aquinas who spoke of sacraments as *protestationes fidei* and with the best strain of traditional Christianity. All this means that it is not a question of liturgical reform *or* spiritual renewal. Both go hand in hand; sacrament and faith are that intertwined.

Liturgical reform, strictly speaking, is directed at making the liturgy, especially the Eucharist, a more powerful sign. That is what the changes in the mass since Vatican II are all about. They have had, it is commonly agreed, mixed success, partly because in a real but complex sense they do not go far enough, but mainly because the church had largely forgotten the sacramental principle: Sacraments signify what they do and they do it because they signify it. Now we always believed the sacraments *worked*, so to speak, but we had lost sight of *how* they work. In fact, the sacramental principle means that they work precisely as signs, that is, as symbolic actions which Christ has given a clear meaning or significance. Symbols, however, are not merely expressive but *constitutive* of experience. And that means, in the case of Christian sacraments, that they are meant not only to express our faith in Christ's saving personal presence in us but to offer intense experience of that presence that can deepen our faith and commitment to him. If they are placid, mechanical signs, administered rather than celebrated, they may actually weaken faith.

General acceptance of the sacramental principle, it is safe to say, however, implies an enormous theological shift for most Catholics. For behind this simple and rather bland-sounding axiom lies the basic Christian assertion that we have generally never dared to take seriously: that in Father Laurentin's words, "human action can become a carrier of the divine, for there is nothing religious which is not, at the same time, human."[2] Christ stands as the supreme example of this revelation and in him its truth is established for us. The latter means that the *whole* of our life, insofar as it is permeated by a living faith, is full of grace: the same word or action mediates the divine as well as the human. That is why the church itself is a sacrament. But the divine is not a sort of easy rider that merely accompanies the human; it transforms it, divinizes it, while leaving it fully human. Fully human, let it be added immediately, not only at home, or in the marketplace, but in church.

The latter has come to be a problem in our time. We gather to celebrate the Eucharist as Christ wished, precisely because our lives, as a result of sin are not fully sacramental; they do not adequately express the divine nor are they for most of us a strong and constant experience of the divine. We need the Eucharist and the other sacraments in order to make the rest of our lives more and more sacramental. To accomplish this the Eucharistic celebration must be fully and authentically human and yet clearly divine; it must, in Laurentin's particularly apt phrase, "express what man is and what God does."[3] If liturgy is to succeed, it must quite simply do both—eloquently. That is the crux of the problem for all who have responsibility for the liturgy. Yet, since Vatican II there has been a tendency to fudge this distinction between liturgy and life in two different ways. Some felt that liturgy ought to be as casual, pedestrian, and ordinary as life: chuck the vestments, use beer and potato chips, trade the Scriptures for Gibran, eliminate anything about the mass that suggests it is more than friends having a meal together. Liturgy ought to be just like life. Others went further, wondering whether there was any point to liturgy at all; life itself was liturgy.

Both views, it should be admitted, have a positive intent which is to stress the value and dignity of the Christian life, and, in the first instance at least, to express the continuity between life and liturgy. They echo the classic Christian affirmation of Augustine in the *City of God* that "a true sacrifice is every work done that we may cleave to God in holy fellowship." In the existential order, however, life is simply not liturgy, not continuously anyway. While liturgy must be fully human, an integral part of culture, this should not be taken to mean that liturgy, in the incisive words of Aelred Tegels, "is simply the sacral projection of a given culture, indiscriminately sanctioning or sanctifying all of its values and institutions. . . . Liturgy is pre-eminently judgment, a transforming, saving encounter with Christ, the supremely classic expression of God's purpose for man."[4] And that, ultimately, is why life requires liturgy to become liturgy. Liturgy is always something more than life, something more than we are at the moment, a celebration of what we hope to become.

Granted the need for liturgy, others have raised the more thoughtful question not about its eloquence but its relevance. Even the reformed Roman liturgy still speaks of shepherds, animals, grain, and vines. It uses ashes, palm, water, salt, oil, candle, and above all bread and wine. Do these things which conjure up visions of a bucolic kind of existence say anything meaningful to the average American Catholic who lives by if not in the city, associates palm with a Florida or Hawaii vacation, and who has never seen a shepherd and never hopes to see one? The question, to tell the truth, was first asked in the early Sixties but is seldom heard any more. Perhaps because in recent years the astronaut, the environmental scientist, and the flower child have awakened in us a new appreciation of the cosmos and we are now more ready, as Pelikan put it, "to celebrate the tenderness and the fierceness of the world" into which the Creator put us. Perhaps too, in a world that to so many seems chaotic, meaningless, and filled with anomie we have sensed with Susanne Langer that "our most important assets are always the symbols of our general orientation in nature, on the earth, in society, and in what we are doing; the symbols of our Weltanschauung and Lebensanschauung."[5] That would seem to mean that we can do very well with the traditional symbolic material of the liturgy if we maximize its power.

That essential task lies largely with the priest not only as celebrant but as the one who summons the community to worship and helps it prepare that experience. Thus he is clearly a crucial part of the sign. He speaks not only to his fellow Christians but for and with them, and not just with his words but through the unspoken yet equally powerful language of his eyes, hands, arms—in short, his whole body. In the old days he *said* mass; in the new liturgy he *celebrates* and draws the community into that action. The medium is much of the message. The priest's faith, warmth, reverence, and joy are to be expressed convincingly not only in the homily but in the whole way he presides—his "presidential style" as it is now called. That, for most of us, does not come naturally; it is an art, something that has to be learned through practice.

Good liturgy, however, requires much more than an expressive celebrant. Especially when the congregation is large, it demands careful, intelligent, creative preparation. And that means preparation with a group, not because two, three, or even ten heads are better than one, not just because it is good for people to feel involved, but mainly because the liturgy must be an honest expression of where the community is as well as of what God asks of it. The liturgy must articulate the faith of the community. That, I am convinced, is the basic reason why priests ought not plan liturgy by themselves; that is also why it might be uncommonly helpful for priests to prepare sermons with a small group. Of course, liturgy committees are also organized to make the Eucharist a robust, meaningful sign. That part of the task is not so easy, nor is it always best accomplished by a committee. It demands not only familiarity with the way symbols work but creativity in manipulating them.

All this suggests that if the general level of liturgy is to improve, it will mean more than designating the youngest priest on the staff as the liturgy director and establishing a parish liturgy committee. Needed is nothing short of a wholehearted decision to make the Sunday Eucharist a clear priority. That implies the willingness to spend money, e.g., to hire a first class musician and install a sound system that is so good that it becomes impossible *not* to hear the Word preached and proclaimed. Just as much, it will involve not just a half hour or so on Saturday evening but an enormous outlay of time for personal preparation, staff discussion, group planning, and the sensitive pastoral care of those who have special roles in the celebration: the lectors, musicians, servers, and not least the ushers. That this would be not only a productive but deeply satisfying commitment may not seem immediately obvious. Why, in view of the fact that the Sunday Eucharist is the only regular contact with the great majority of adult Catholics, it is not more generally undertaken does not seem obvious at all.

Still, Rome and the National Catholic Conference of Bishops could help. Much can be done with the liturgy as it is but further changes are in order. A good case in point is the liturgy of the word; three readings interspersed by two songs[6] that are seldom sung. Three readings is one, perhaps two, too many. The Scriptures are meant to be heard, understood, and absorbed. That is almost impossible when the context is abruptly switched within five minutes or so and the congregation is enlisted to enter on cue with a verse of psalm. It is a splendid sequence on paper, but it doesn't come off in reality. Words become sounds; the readings a formality to be endured until attention returns (sometimes only momentarily) at the start of the homily. To some extent this illustrates a basic fault in the new liturgy, or perhaps better, the way it is often presented. It is too much work, too full of words (even our banners), often too much like a lesson. Not enough song, nonverbal symbols, and silence. As someone a few years ago described the situation with delicious precision, "We have exchanged our birthright for a pot of message." Admittedly, the situation could be markedly improved at the local level but a radical change in the structure of this part of the liturgy would be even better.

Something else that needs attention is the Eucharistic prayer. It is a blessing we have four, two of which have a considerable variety of prefaces. Nonetheless, a problem arises, not just from this rather limited selection, nor from the way this central statement of the meaning of the Eucharist is sometimes "proclaimed," eyes glued to the page as though following a recipe, voice droning out the words in a seemingly unimpressed monotone. The eucharistic prayers as they now stand are cluttered; their basic movement from praise and thanksgiving to offering, and the invocation of the Spirit is not, except in the case of Prayer IV, readily discernible. The impression obtained is one of an amorphous collage of prayers with the institution narrative stuck in the middle.

Such improvements would take a little doing. What could be done immediately, however, is to introduce some changes in the Communion rite. It's time, I think, for the church to shed all hesitancy about Communion under both species. That should be a principle not a privilege. One should have to have reasons for *not* communicating the congregation under both species and not the other way around. I am not calling for new regulations but an unequivocal statement that Communion under its full sign is the *ideal*. That might encourage priests to arrange things so that it would be more generally possible.

What does not seem generally possible in the foreseeable future, at least on a weekly basis, is small group Eucharistic celebration. In recent years any number of voices have arisen to argue that this mode of celebration best reflects and effects the unique closeness of mutual concern that should characterize a Christian community. The quality of New Testament *koinonia* can only be strained at masses whose congregations are large and inevitably anonymous. Well, maybe. It is certainly a fact that many people have had the most profound experience of what it means to be church at a home mass when all the participants were known to each other. It is also true that mass seems to mean more when you're with, or at least see, someone you know. I would argue, though, that at the Eucharist what we need even more than each other's name is a lively sense of each other's faith. That faith must be perceived to embrace the Real Presence not only on the altar but in the community and in the world beyond. It is communicated by participation in community song and prayer, alert attention, posture, facial expression and a hundred little ways. It effects a climate of reverence without stiffness, warmth without coziness, and joy without hilarity. Faith so expressed covers a multitude of worshipers; it effectively dissipates anonymity.

In fact, however, a multitude for liturgy, if by that is meant "temple liturgy"—Eucharist celebrated with unusual splendor—is a positive necessity, *occasionally*. It can revitalize the house or small group liturgy which, as Lauretin points out, "runs the risk of being content with the horizontal, with warm and generous sentiments, and so gives up the 'beyond

in the midst' which is no less necessary for authentic celebration."[7] However, the trouble, for the present, is that the
average Sunday Eucharist often falls somewhere in between:
It lacks the intimacy and spontaneity of small group celebration and the eloquence of the other. Sheer numbers are a
large part of the problem. Ultimately, I suspect that means
more celebrations, and probably more celebrants. In the
meantime, things could be helped by modification of the
canonical principle of the territorial parish. Rahner is right,
I think, when he scores inflexibility in the interpretation of
this principle as a kind of "ecclesiastical state socialism"
which, in the present age especially, can be detrimental to
genuine pastoral care. *Let my people go.* As a matter of fact,
some of them are going, though not without feeling guilty.
That could be alleviated if priests more generally recognized
the need, faced their human problem of rejection, and
worked out, after consultation with the people and with the
bishop's support, a solution motivated by the same pastoral
concern that formerly made the territorial principle an appropriate absolute.

One last problem for church authorities is the notoriously
delicate matter of intercommunion. Before Vatican II it did
not exist. While the Eucharist had always been understood
as the sign of the unity of the church, the latter term for all
practical purposes applied exclusively to the Roman Catholic
church. The immense theological shift of Vatican II, which
highlighted the invisible nature of the church, broke that
monopoly. The Council recognized that the Spirit was alive
and active not only in Orthodox but Protestant bodies which
it called "ecclesial communities." This long overdue bit of
noblesse oblige has led to the shattering of old theological

deadlocks over the real presence, the sacrificial nature of the Eucharist, and the potential of the sacraments for signifying a more perfect unity to be achieved. According to some theologians only one barrier keeps Catholic and some Protestant churches from full intercommunion: mutual recognition of their valid ministry. On the Catholic side even this appears to be caving in with theologians abandoning the old canonical concept of validity of orders in favor of the criterion of de facto fidelity to the New Testament image of ministry. However, not a few would simply second the straightforward conclusion of Charles Meyer:

> From a strictly theological viewpoint, if the Eucharist is the nourishment of the initial union between Christ and Christians effected by baptism and not the sign of a more perfect kind of union, there is no real problem about intercommunion. If the Eucharist as a sacrament is the sign of the inner union of grace rather than of the external bonds of church or ecclesial community, the chief objection against intercommunion vanishes. Opponents of this practice who challenge it on theological grounds must consider the bond it effects a more perfect one than that of baptism: but tradition acknowledges only one bond: that of baptism, which the Eucharist refurbishes and nurtures.[8]

The Secretariat for Promoting Christian Unity, which speaks for the Pope in these matters, has not been so bold. In one recent pronouncement on the admission of other Christians to the Catholic Eucharist it went beyond its 1967 directive but clearly stated the practice must be considered "exceptional," i.e., limited to situations when such Christians found themselves in grave spiritual need and without a possibility of recourse to their own communities.

Interfaith practice in many areas of this country as well as others, however, has gone far behind the new guidelines, which may suggest we're ready for something more. Just the same, most theologians who disallow any theological objection to intercommunion are careful to point out the important existential factors like ignorance, suspicion, and fear which would contraindicate any simple "Open Door" policy. Father Lash whose approach is always markedly pastoral, would even continue to prohibit intercommunion at ecumenical gatherings because "serious disunity within one or more churches seems a high price to pay for the occasional sacramental expression of unity among the ecumenically alert."[9] His recommendation is an ever deepening collaboration in life, work, and witness as a prelude to sharing the Eucharist. There is, I think, more to be done than that. Catholics and Protestants had better become much more familiar with the richness of their own traditions so that they might not be undone when and if intercommunion becomes more general. If all that we have said in recent years about the specific genius of particular segments of Christianity was not just polite talk, then those several gifts should not be lost in a pallid ecumenism that misinterprets uniformity for unity. We have one faith, one Lord, one baptism; what concrete forms that unity should assume in the future is the Spirit's to know and ours to find out. I cannot believe he wishes to eliminate all ecclesial diversity. That would suggest the Reformation was only a punishment, not a purification.

For that reason I am not unhappy with the Vatican's characterization of intercommunion as "exceptional." To disengage the Eucharist altogether from the concrete reality of one's own faith community strikes me as unreal. Nonetheless, "exceptional" doesn't have to mean "hardly ever," in effect, never. Granted the faith, sincerity, and mutual respect of the people involved and with the consent of their communities, formally expressed through their leaders, might not both the unity and diversity of the one Body of Christ be fruitfully celebrated in a shared Eucharist on certain special occasions? Under these conditions I do not think scandal or serious dis- unity need arise, say, if intercommunion were allowed at least for the bride and groom at interfaith weddings or even for certain kinds of ecumenical gatherings. There is legitimate precedent at least for the former. There are serious people asking for both. Enough probably for bishops and the leaders of other Christian churches to explore the question again.

Intercommunion, however, is obviously not the central problem of the church. Faith is, was, and always will be. And while the Eucharist has immense power to augment faith it cannot substitute for its absence. There was a short-lived tendency to forget this in the years immediately following Vatican II but that particular naivete appears to be behind us. What that renewal will entail is beyond the scope of this little essay, but it is certain that it will involve the traditional concern with prayer, aseticism, and charity. And in this age of mass media and vastly increased social consciousness it means those must not remain simply private virtues but con- stitute the profile of the church as a whole and particularly its leadership.

Is this possible? It's happening. In many corners of the world, in many people. One has only to remember what the church was like twenty-five years ago. Who would want to return? A few perhaps. But the church is now much less a law and order church, much more expressive of the gospel spirit of freedom, justice and love. It has emerged shaken by a decade of unprecedented reform but is slowly coming to understand what the interiorization of that reform will demand. It has begun to discover what it means to be *in* rather than apart from history; it has become more tolerant of its past, responsive to the present, and more hopeful in contemplating its future. If it is less complacent with its present state, it senses, at least in part, that its standards are higher, its vision elevated. It is learning to accept, if not yet appreciate, the tensions within as a sign of life and the opportunity for growth. Where hope ultimately lies, however, is in the fact that while it is not yet free of the arrogance that is revealed in its disinclination at various times and places to practice the discernment of spirits, the church does more resolutely believe that the Spirit is the source of its life and that the same Spirit hovers over it, and indeed, the whole world "with ah! bright wings."

NOTES

Chapter One

1. *In illo tempore:* literally, *at that time.* This phrase introduced every mass gospel until the first Sunday of Advent, 1964.

2. John Jankauskas, *Our Tongues were Loosed.* Westminster: The Newman Press, 1965.

Chapter Two

1. Andrew Greeley, *What a Modern Catholic Believes about the Church.* The Thomas More Press: Chicago, Illinois, 1972. St. Ursula is the pseudonym Father Greeley uses for the parish of his youth: a typical immigrant parish of the thirties.

2. *Ibid,* p. 75.

3. J. A. Jungmann, S.J., "Church Art," *Worship,* XXXIX, No. 2. (January, 1955), 68–82.

4. In English, Christ is "true God and true man."

5. The plural form is introduced at this time by St. Isidore. This innovation signals a shift in the understanding of the word.

6. Quoted by Archbishop Paul Hallinan, "Towards a People's Liturgy, *Worship,* Vol. 42, No. 5, May, 1968 (258–263) p. 258.

Chapter Three

1. Aidan Kavanaugh's happy phrase, "Relevance and Change in the Liturgy": *Worship,* Vol. 45, No. 2, February, 1971, pp. 58–72, p. 62.

2. One solidly probable opinion, however, maintained that less than three White Castle hamburgers did not constitute grave matter.

3. Charles Meyer, *A Contemporary Theology of Grace* (Staten Island, N.Y.: Alba House, 1970), p. 106.

4. Saul Bellow, *Mr. Sammler's Planet.* (New York: The Viking Press, 1970), p. 228.

5. Rev. Louis Bouyer, *Rite and Man.* Notre Dame: University of Notre Dame Press, 1963, p. 66.

Chapter Four

1. Italics supplied.

2. Rev. Josef A. Jungmann, S.J., *The Mass of the Roman Rite.* New York: Benziger Brothers, Inc., 1953, Vol. II, p. 378.

Chapter Five

1. Henri DeLubac, S.J., *The Splendour of the Church.* (New York: Sheed and Ward, 1956, pp. 110–111.

2. Meyer, *Theology of Grace,* p. 38.

3. Nicholas Lash, *His Presence in the World.* (Dayton: Pflaum Press, 1968), p. 171.

4. Edward J. Kilmartin, S.J., "The Eucharist in Recent Literature," *Theological Studies,* Vol. 32, No. 2 (June, 1971), pp. 233–277.

5. *Ibid.*

Chapter Six

1. Karl Rahner, S.J., *The Christian Commitment* (New York: Sheed and Ward, 1963), pp. 139–140.

2. Andre Laurentin, "Theatre and Liturgy," *Worship,* Vol. 43, No. 7 (August-September, 1969), p. 395.

3. *Ibid.*

4. Aelred Tegels, "Liturgy and Culture: Adaptation or Symbiosis?" *Worship,* Vol. 41, No. 6 (June-July, 1967), pp. 364–372.

5. Susanne K. Langer, *Philosophy in a New Key.* (New York: Mentor Books, 1951), pp. 241–2.

6. What could be more absurd than 1000 people rising to *say* Alleluia, alleluia, alleluia?

7. Laurentin, *op. cit.,* p. 405.

8. Meyer, *Theology of Grace,* pp. 41–42.

9. Lash, *op. cit.,* p. 200.